Backcountry
COCKTAILS

LAND ACKNOWLEDGMENT

The geographical heart of this book is the White Mountains of New Hampshire, part of N'dakinna, the traditional ancestral homeland of the Abenaki, Pennacook, and Wabanaki peoples past and present. We acknowledge and honor with gratitude the land and waterways and the alnobak (people) who have stewarded N'dakinna throughout the generations.

Backcountry COCKTAILS

CIVILIZED DRINKS FOR WILD PLACES

Inspired by the White Mountains

STEVEN GRASSE
& ADAM ERACE

with LEE NOBLE

RUNNING PRESS
PHILADELPHIA

Running Press
Hachette Book Group
1290 Avenue of the Americas, New York, NY 10104
www.runningpress.com
@Running_Press

Printed in China

First Edition: May 2023

Published by Running Press, an imprint of Perseus Books, LLC, a subsidiary of Hachette Book Group, Inc. The Running Press name and logo are trademarks of the Hachette Book Group.

The publisher is not responsible for websites (or their content) that are not owned by the publisher.

LCCN: 2022022314

ISBNs: 978-0-7624-8054-8 (hardcover), 978-0-7624-8055-5 (ebook)

1010

10 9 8 7 6 5 4 3 2 1

Contents

Greetings from the
WHITE
MOUNTAINS

The White Mountain National Forest of New Hampshire is one of the most beautiful natural places in the country, comprising 750,000 acres of majestic snow-covered peaks, mirror-like lakes, and dense mythic woods domed by skies so dark the constellations glow like stadium lights. Its lacework of waterways and ancient forests bursting with life sustained Indigenous peoples for millennia, and after colonization, authors, artists, and adventurers both bygone and contemporary have sought and found inspiration in this epic environment.

The White Mountains are the spiritual heart of *Backcountry Cocktails*, but this book is not a travel guide, souvenir, or keepsake just for folks who reside or vacation here. Rather, we want the area to serve as a state of mind, a four-seasons stand-in for any wild place where you might find yourself in need of a quality cocktail: a starlit bonfire at an off-grid campsite, a hygge ski chalet booked on Airbnb, a hike through a national park, or the deck of a vintage Chris-Craft that gleams like a wooden rocket across a secret lake whose location is passed down like a family heirloom. Outdoor places. And indoor places whose whole reason for being is the outdoors.

Our cocktail expertise flows from the historic town of Tamworth, located at the doorstep of the White Mountains. There, on the grounds of the town's old inn and theater, we make spirits from scratch at Tamworth Distilling with house-milled grain, pure mountain water, herbs and botanicals from the woods and our garden, local fruits and vegetables, and other wild treasures like raw honey, foraged black trumpet mushrooms (see Field Guide: Wild Mushrooms, page 116), venison, and beaver musk (see Hunter's Stew, page 104)—which tastes like raspberries and vanilla, if you can believe it. The Tamworth approach marries innovation and experimentation with deep interest in and reverence for the land. Our recipes are born from the crops we grow and the histories buried in the soil below.

You could say the same about the cocktails forming the bulk of this book. There are forty-eight in total, twelve for each season, which will carry you from the vernal buds of Spring to the whiteouts of Winter. Each is an original creation or outdoors-minded twist on a classic. Which brings us to the question you're probably wondering about . . .

What Makes a BACKCOUNTRY COCKTAIL?

Backcountry *(noun)*: sparsely inhabited rural areas; wilderness
—*Oxford Languages Dictionary*

Almost everyone loves the outdoors, but *actual* outdoorsiness exists on a very wide spectrum. Maybe you're an off-the-grid backpacker. Or maybe your idea of roughing it includes Wi-Fi, fireplaces, and weighted blankets. We respect that! And it's why inclusiveness and versatility are the North Stars of this cocktail collection. In whichever capacity you feel comfortable connecting with the wild, we'll meet you there, with a drink in hand.

So what exactly constitutes a Backcountry Cocktail? Well, here are a few examples:

• A portable bottle of green juice spiked with mezcal and chile liqueur
  (Hiker's Lament, page 14)
• A refreshing take on summer fruit (White Port Peach Cobbler, page 66)
• A batched negroni steeped with cinnamon sticks (Cinnegroni, page 115)
• A gather 'round cauldron of Chartreuse hot chocolate (Alpine Cocoa, page 140)

In personality and format, these are very different drinks, but they're all Backcountry Cocktails—civilized drinks inspired by or created for wild places. In the pages that follow you'll encounter concoctions purpose-built for camping, traveling, and outdoor living, like the Ameri-can-o (page 80) and Maple Slush (page 153), as well as ones that might feel more at home in the cozy cocoon of a cabin, like the American Eclipse (page 17) or Flannel Sheets (page 150). That said, there isn't one recipe in this book that you can make in one setting but can't in the other, so if you want to carry in a set of coupes to your campsite, proceed with our blessing and perpetual admiration. Below, find some other parameters we considered when creating the cocktails for this book.

BATCHABLE AND PACKABLE

Of the recipes, about half are one-liquor drinks and about a third are two-liquor drinks, to minimize the number of heavy bottles you'll have to pack. Moreso, we developed these cocktails to be easily scaled up and batched out in advance, if you'd rather premix at home before heading out on a trip. Glass canning jars and deli containers are your best friends for this. Be sure to leave any fizzy ingredients out until you're ready to serve.

HOMEMADE BASICS

Browning butter, toasting spices, brewing tea, infusing simple syrups—a Backcountry Cocktail won't ask you to do anything more complicated than that. Every homemade component can be prepared on-site with indoor or outdoor heat sources, or simply made ahead of time.

COOLER CONSCIOUS

Cold storage can be at a premium when traveling outside of Winter. With just one exception (Alpine Cocoa, page 140), expect to see us call for canned coconut and sweetened condensed milks, which are shelf-stable and a cinch to pack, rather than fresh milk or cream. Fizzes and sours (Violet Fizz, page 22; Blackberry Basil Sour, page 65) call for egg whites, for which aquafaba is a fine (and vegan) alternative. Whole eggs in the Jack-O'-Lantern (page 137) and Coconut Hamp Nog (page 168) are harder to replace, since they add important richness and body to those cocktails. If traveling with a dozen feels like an impending disaster, batch these two out ahead of time, but be sure to keep them cold.

EASY ICE AND GLASSWARE

Speaking of cooler consciousness, ice can be a real space hog. Many cocktail books call for lots of different types of ice—hell, we wrote one, *The Cocktail Workshop*—but in this context, save yourself the headache by using standard cubes for mixing and serving. For drinks that call for crushed ice (Mont Blanc, page 174; White Port Peach Cobbler, page 66), use a freezer bag and something heavy to make your own. Similarly, packing lots of different glassware makes no sense, so we kept the selection tight: tall and short glasses, mugs, and coupes. But by all means, use what you've got: a Mason jar, a thermos, a hollowed-out gourd. The point is the drink inside, not what it's served in.

WILD ADDITIONS

We'll highlight ingredients that can be harvested from the wild, like strawberries in the Forager's Smash (page 13) or sumac in the Mack Rose (page 97), but we recognize what's growing here may not be growing there, and that scrounging around in the woods is not everyone's idea of a good time. Substitutions where sensible are listed in the recipes. The Blue Bee G&T (page 90) made with rosemary instead of spruce tips, for example, won't taste exactly the same, but it will still be damn delicious.

SPECIALTY INGREDIENTS AND SUBSTITUTIONS

Backcountry Cocktails rely on drink-making staples: whiskey, gin, rum, mint, lemon, bitters, seltzer, and so on, but sometimes sourcing and packing an extra item, like Zirbenz pine liqueur for the Pine Collins (page 167), is truly necessary. When a recipe goes beyond the basics, we'll often list a reasonable substitution, like using bottled birch beer instead of birch syrup in the Bark and Stormy (page 75) or recreating the Damson Negroni's (page 161) plum gin with plain gin and preserves.

FUN AND FLEXIBILITY ABOVE ALL

Please remember: It's just drinks! These cocktails are here to complement and enhance an experience in the great outdoors, never overtake it. Safe travels and happy mixing!

Your Guides

The drinks are the raison d'être of *Backcountry Cocktails*. But we didn't want to make just another drinks book. Our goal is to get you, dear reader, to engage and connect more deeply with nature, which is why peppered throughout the chapters you'll find heaps of wilderness-relevant information: illustrated instructionals on building a fire (page 142), preserving fruit (page 68), and other skills; field guides to wild flora; and recipes for simple, delicious food you can cook indoors or out. From the White Mountains and beyond, several experts contributed their backcountry expertise to these pages. Please meet your guides.

STEVE BARTLETT, *Booty Family Farm*

Steve Bartlett married into maple. "My wife's parents were back-to-the-land hippies who bought a one-hundred-year-old farm that had completely disintegrated into the earth, Robert Frost–style, and revitalized it." Located in the town of Sandwich, New Hampshire, Booty Family Farm deals in organic vegetables, logging, and, during the Winter and early Spring, maple syrup. "We run about three hundred or so buckets during the sugaring season," which boils down (literally) into seventy to two hundred gallons of finished syrup, depending on the year. "While there's a lot of variability in quantity, one thing you can always depend on: The sap will run."

Further reading: How to: Tap a Maple (page 154)

JAMAAR JULAL,
JamBrü Ferments and *Honeysuckle Projects*

In just a couple of years, Jamaar Julal has gone from scrubbing volatile experiments off his ceiling to running a rapidly expanding kombucha line and serving as director of fermentation for Honeysuckle Projects, a food-focused community center, market, and farm in Philadelphia. "What I love about fermentation is the limitlessness; when I first began to learn about fermentation, I had no idea how expansive it truly is or how integrated into my life it already was," says Jamaar, who's also a professionally trained chef and avid forager who transforms wild edibles into various fermentations.

Further reading: How to: Ferment Veggies (page 46); Lion's Mane "Crab Cakes" with Fermented-Ramp Tartar Sauce (page 120)

ANTON KASKA,
Borealis Traders of New England

A newspaper article, devoured while waiting for a ride home from the airport after a business trip to Spain, changed Anton Kaska's life trajectory. After twenty-one years overseas, including a decade with the army, the security and communications specialist settled in New Hampshire, a state simpatico with his individualistic streak. And so the proposed legislation to ban trapping, as outlined in the article, rankled him. "I didn't trap, but I didn't think it was right all this outside money was coming in trying to change how people live." There was a town hall to discuss the matter in an hour and a half. Instead of going home, Anton went to the meeting in Concord and spoke against the ban. "Some trappers came up to me after, like, 'Thanks, but who are you?'" Anton was still in his suit; they thought he was representing the other side. "Next thing I knew, I was in the state's trapper education class." Now, when the wildlife service needs a dammed pond diverted, black foxes to study the effectiveness of rabies vaccination programs, or vicious fishers (a weasel relative) relocated a safe distance from neighborhood doggy doors and chicken coops, they call Anton.
Further reading: Field Guide: Deer Tracking (page 128), Hunter's Stew (page 104)

ERIC MILLIGAN,
New Hampshire Mushroom Company

A theater major with a background in industrial engineering, Eric Milligan came to mushrooms accidentally, falling down the fungi hole while rehabbing a broken leg with slow walks in the woods. "I started studying mycology in 2005, and it quickly turned into an obsession with all things fungi. Seven years year, New Hampshire Mushroom Company was born." In addition to cultivating specialty mushrooms for home cooks and chefs, Eric leads classes in mycological identification, cooking, crafting, medicine, and more.
Further reading: Field Guide: Wild Mushrooms (page 116)

ERIC MORRIS, *N.onT.ypical Outdoorsman*

What gives Eric Morris's wilderness web series its nontypical branding? The cross-country hunter, mentor, and army veteran's commitment to doing things the old-fashioned way. "Because of developments in technology, I think a lot of us are losing the fundamentals of hunting. It doesn't take a lot of gadgets and gizmos," only a bow, spear, or shotgun. Eric hunts for food, not sport: squirrel, deer, quail, pheasant, bear, and more. "Basically if it breathes, flies, or swims, I'll hunt it."

Further reading: How to: Scare a Bear (page 36)

LEE NOBLE, *Tamworth Distilling*

Before he became the mixology maestro for Tamworth Distilling and its Philadelphia brother businesses, Art in the Age and Quaker City Mercantile, Lee Noble was a backcountry canoe camping guide in the "very remote" boundary waters of Minnesota, north of Lake Superior. "No roads in, no motor traffic, no flyover—unless it was a plane on a rescue mission." The best way to avoid an emergency airlift? Basic wilderness skills, which Lee would teach his campers. In a way, it's not so different from what he does now. "Sometimes I have to show absolute novices how to manage a situation, whether it's how to make a campfire or make a cocktail."

Further reading: How to: Pack a Cooler (page 58), How to: Pitch a Tent (page 84), How to: Build a Fire (page 142), How to: Traverse a Beaver Dam (page 102)

MJ PETTENGILL, *Marigold Moon Wildcraft Apothecary*

"If you want to get my attention, fire up the lawnmower." Mj Pettengill, whose Marigold Moon Wildcraft Apothecary is a fairytale cottage in the Sandwich, New Hampshire, woods, will "run to the window, yelling, *NO!*" Where others see weeds, the author, educator, and pharmacist of flora sees the building blocks of potions both medicinal and delectable. "This area is just so abundant with healing plants. To use them is to honor the land, literally connecting with our roots through these roots."

Further reading: Field Guide: Medicinal Plants (page 18), Dandelion Wine (page 20)

DENISE AND PAUL POULIOT,
Cowasuck Band of the Pennacook-Abenaki People

As the Sag8moskwa (head female speaker) and Sag8mo (head male speaker) of the Cowasuck Band of the Pennacook-Abenaki people, Denise and Paul Pouliot serve the community on several state and regional alliances dealing with race, equality, food insecurity, sustainability, education, climate change, social services, and justice related to marginalized and BIPOC communities, including the Indigenous New Hampshire Collaborative Collective. Part of this work is preserving culture through food and drink. "We Indigenize recipes," Paul says, winding them back to reflect the ingredients that would have been available to Native cooks prior to colonization, "like sumac, which we use in lieu of lemon."

Further reading: Succotash (page 130), Pemmigan (page 158)

Spring

FORAGER'S SMASH

You spot them by your feet, like little red gumdrops on the ground—wild strawberries. On a late-spring walk through the woods, there are few greater rewards than discovering a cache of these rubies. *Fragaria vesca* and *Fragaria virginiana*, the two common varieties of wild strawberry, are hard to come by, but you only need to collect a half dozen to make a memorable springtime smash. This old-timey, fruit-festooned cocktail is akin to a mint julep, but our vodka-based version feels closer in spirit to a mojito. The Forager's Smash comes together quickly: Just muddle all the ingredients together right in the glass, pack it with ice, garnish, and go. If you can't source the ginger vodka, just add two sturdy slices of fresh ginger to the muddling mix or make your own by combining fresh smashed ginger, a touch of sugar, and neutral vodka in a sturdy container for a week, then straining and bottling the infusion.

MAKES 1 COCKTAIL

2 ounces / 60 ml Tamworth or other ginger vodka

8 large mint leaves

6 wild strawberries (substitute 3 medium or large store-bought, halved lengthwise)

1 sugar cube

Garnish: Mint sprig, strawberry wheel

Gently muddle the vodka, mint, berries, and sugar in the bottom of a short glass. Fill the glass with ice and stir until the sugar is completely dissolved. Top off with more ice if necessary, garnish, and serve.

HIKER'S LAMENT

We've all been there: A night around the campfire goes a little too late. The cooler gets a little more depleted than it should. The sun comes a little too early, and that dawn hike that sounded like a spectacular idea yesterday now feels like a savage punishment. Here's a detox/retox to bring you back to life: Green juice (store-bought or homemade, your call) dosed with mezcal and chile liqueur. It's invigorating, spicy, nutritious, and not very high in alcohol, plus you make it right in the bottle. Give the Hiker's Lament about half an hour to chill before drinking, or better yet, make one up the night before.

MAKES 1 COCKTAIL

1 bottle (12 to 15 ounces / 370 to 440 ml) green juice of choice, chilled

1½ ounces / 45 ml mezcal

¾ ounce / 22 ml Ancho Reyes Verde chile poblano liqueur

Pinch kosher salt

Open the bottle of juice and take two big sips. Add the mezcal, chile liqueur, and salt to the bottle, close the bottle, and shake to combine. Chill for 30 minutes before serving.

AMERICAN ECLIPSE

Modeled on the Eclipse from *Drinks—Long and Short*, published in London in 1925, the American Eclipse pushes the vague but promising recipe of "Four glasses of rum, one glass of Chartreuse and one of sweetened lemon juice. Serve with a cherry" into a more complex cocktail that's as pale green as a newborn leaf. How does that happen? First, respect the unlikely power couple of rum and Chartreuse. Second, replace the lemon with pineapple, which is more interesting, and sweeten it with falernum, a whole damn spice rack distilled into a handy syrup. The result is a sophisticated drink with a tropical vibe that's very well suited to early Spring, aka Mud Season, when the obstinate cold and mess-making snowmelt necessitate a reminder of balmier days ahead.

MAKES 1 COCKTAIL

2 ounces / 60 ml light rum

½ ounce / 15 ml green Chartreuse

½ ounce / 15 ml pineapple juice

½ ounce / 15 ml falernum syrup

Garnish: Cherry

Combine the rum, Chartreuse, pineapple juice, and falernum in a shaker with ice, vigorously shake, and strain the cocktail into a chilled coupe. Garnish and serve.

Field Guide:
MEDICINAL PLANTS
BY MJ PETTENGILL

Nature hurts and nature heals. For every nasty wasp sting, brush with poison ivy, unexpected cold snap, or storm of pollen, there's a plant to help. Here are six of the most common springtime healers. As always, exercise caution when foraging and consuming wild plants, and in serious circumstances, seek professional medical attention.

BROADLEAF PLANTAIN, *PLANTAGO MAJOR*

A common edible weed and effective wound healer found in lawns, driveways, parks, and sandy disturbed soil, broadleaf plantain is easy to identify by the five parallel veins running lengthwise on each leaf. Applied as a poultice to bee stings and other bug bites, a chewed-up plantain leaf stops itching and reduces swelling.

WOODLAND VIOLETS, *VIOLA SORORIA*

Packed with minerals and vitamins, specifically A and C, violet flowers, leaves, and stems are nutritious immune boosters. They make a great trail snack, are excellent raw in salads or steamed with other greens, and when infused into Honey Syrup (see Blue Bee G&T, page 90) create a natural sore throat soother.

YARROW ROOT, *ACHILLEA MILLEFOLIUM*

The manifold benefits of this sturdy flowering herb, a member of the sunflower family, earned it the nickname soldier's woundwort for its centuries of use on battlefields. If you're looking for an application more pertinent to camping than war, chewing its peppery root eases tooth pain, a godsend while far from the nearest dentist. Find it in grassy fields, along the edges of established gardens, and in disturbed soil.

DANDELION, *TARAXACUM OFFICINALE*

This easily recognized, prolific weed not only makes exceptional wine (see Dandelion Wine, page 20), but its root and leaves can also be brewed into a tea to strengthen and tonify the liver—useful if you need to deal with an overload of allergens and toxins that cause the body to produce histamines. It is abundant and grows in fields and garden spaces everywhere.

CHICKWEED, *STELLARIA MEDIA*

Rich in vitamin C and potassium, chickweed is known to rejuvenate the skin, providing a cooling and drying effect on minor burns, eczema, psoriasis, and other common skin inflammations. For topical use, create a salve from the plant's essential oils. Find chickweed in both abandoned and current garden beds in the early Spring.

WILD ROSE HIPS, *ROSA CANINA*

The accessory fruit of the rosebush, these round red-orange bulbs are full of vitamins C, A, B3, D, and E as well as bioflavonoids and minerals. The density of vitamin C in particular makes rose-hip tea a common natural preventative and treatment for the common cold.

DANDELION WINE

Of the hundreds of tinctures, teas, and tonics that fill the shelves of her Marigold Moon Wildcraft Apothecary, Dandelion Wine might be the elixir Mj Pettengill loves the most. She brews this sweet, centuries-old fermentation in late Spring, when the dandelions explode in profuse yellow pom-poms. For her recipe, you must harvest only freshly blossomed, never wilted, plants—you'll have the best luck in the morning—and hand-pluck the petals from the flower heads, leaving behind as much green as possible to avoid unwanted bitterness.

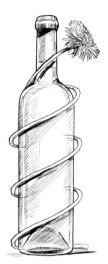

MAKES ABOUT 1 GALLON / 3.8 L

2 quarts / 200 g wild dandelion flowers

1 gallon / 3.8 L filtered water

Juice and zest of 3 lemons

Juice and zest of 3 oranges

1½ pounds / 680 g granulated sugar

¾ pound / 340 g golden raisins, chopped

1 teaspoon yeast nutrient

1 (5 gram) packet wine yeast

Simple Syrup (optional, see Violet Fizz, page 22)

Wash the flowers and let them air-dry completely. Pluck the petals from the flower heads, being careful to leave any green leaves behind. Add the petals to a large, heatproof container. Bring the water to a boil in a large pot. Pour it over the flowers and allow the mixture to steep for 4 hours.

Line a large sieve with cheesecloth and strain the infusion into a large pot. Bundle the cheesecloth up around the flowers and wring it well to extract as much liquid as possible. Set the infusion over high heat and bring it to a boil. Quickly add the lemon and orange juices and sugar and stir to completely dissolve. Add the lemon and orange zests and the raisins and remove the pot from the heat. Occasionally stir the mixture as it cools to room temperature, then transfer to a large heatproof container. Add the yeast nutrient and wine yeast and thoroughly stir. Securely cover and allow the mixture to sit at room temperature for 12 days, stirring 3 times a day.

After 12 days, strain the mixture into a cleaned and sterilized 1 gallon / 3.8 L jug or vessel. Seal it with a fermentation lock and allow it to ferment at room temperature for 21 days.

After 21 days, carefully pour the mixture into another cleaned and sterilized secondary fermentation vessel of the same size, leaving the sediments from the yeast and other ingredients at the bottom of the first vessel, allowing for clear wine. If there is a gap greater than 2 inches / 5 cm between the wine and the rim of the jug, add Simple Syrup, bringing it to 1/2 inch / 1.3 cm from the top. Seal it with a fermentation lock and allow the wine to ferment at room temperature for another 30 days. If desired, continue to repeat this process every month until the wine looks completely clear.

You can consume the wine immediately—store it in cleaned and sterilized glass jars—but the flavor improves when aged at least a year. For long-term storage, funnel the wine into cleaned and sterilized bottles and firmly cork. Store the wine in a cool, dark place and serve at cellar temperature.

VIOLET FIZZ

Violets are among the forest's first wildflowers to bloom—tiny invitations of purple splashed with yellow and white. This featherweight cocktail captures that ephemeral moment of Spring, introducing the subtle fragrance and flavor of violets into a classic gin fizz format. Go with a botanical gin here (Hendrick's, Uncle Val's) rather than an assertive London dry style (Beefeater, Tanqueray) to complement rather than overwhelm the delicate florals. Egg whites are traditional in a fizz, but it's also fine to drop them, turning the recipe into a Violet Collins.

MAKES 1 COCKTAIL

1 ounce / 30 ml gin

1 ounce / 30 ml crème de violette

½ ounce / 15 ml freshly squeezed lime juice

½ ounce / 15 ml Simple Syrup

White from 1 large egg or
1 ounce / 30 ml aquafaba

Seltzer to top, about 1 ounce / 30 ml

Garnish: 3 drops violet or lavender bitters (optional)

Combine the gin, crème de violette, lime juice, syrup, and egg white in a shaker and vigorously shake to whip the egg white. Add ice and shake again. Strain into a tall glass, top with the seltzer, garnish, and serve.

SIMPLE SYRUP

MAKES 1 CUP / 240 ML

¾ cup / 180 ml water

¾ cup / 150 g granulated sugar

Bring the water to a boil in a small pot on the stove, grill, or campfire. Remove the pot from the heat, add the sugar, and stir to completely dissolve. Allow the finished syrup to cool, transfer it to a jar, and store cold until ready to use.

GREAT CARBUNCLE

Eight adventurers set off on a quest for a dazzling scarlet gem in "The Great Carbuncle," one of Nathaniel Hawthorne's short stories inspired by his travels in the White Mountains. (Spoiler alert: The earnest "young bride" and her husband find the fiery jewel but prudently leave it be.) In honor of the tale, here's another Carbuncle, a refresher you *won't* be able to leave alone. It's a riff on the quill, which is itself an absinthe-kissed riff on the negroni, and it's as sparkling and red as the legendary stone. The won't-quit fizz comes from sour cherry lambic, a sweet and tart beer style from Belgium. Lindemans, the lambic brewery most available in the US, produces the sweet Kriek and the more complex Oude Kriek Cuvée René, both of which work beautifully in this recipe.

MAKES 1 COCKTAIL

1½ ounces / 45 ml Aperol

¼ ounce / 7 ml anisette

3 ounces / 90 ml sour cherry lambic

Garnish: Cherry

Combine the Aperol and anisette in a short glass with ice and briskly stir to combine. Top with the lambic and gently stir just to incorporate. Garnish and serve.

"Nor could the young bride any longer deny that a radiance was breaking through the mist, and changing its dim hue to a dusky red, which continually grew more vivid, as if brilliant particles were interfused with the gloom. [. . .] The simple pair had reached that lake of mystery, and found the long-sought shrine of the Great Carbuncle!"—**"'The Great Carbuncle': A Mystery of the White Mountains," Nathaniel Hawthorne, 1835**

SELERY COCKTAIL

Tall, effervescent, and borderline fluorescent, the Selery Cocktail embodies the bright, verdant, regenerative nature of Spring. The name nods to celery, of course, but also the salinity that keeps every sip of this drink sharp and incredibly refreshing. There's actual salt in the mix and garnish, as well as gose, the tart and saline German style of beer, and manzanilla, whose briny terroir comes from its origins on the Atlantic coast of Spain. On a warm afternoon in May, this is the cocktail you want to crush all day.

MAKES 1 COCKTAIL

2 ounces / 60 ml manzanilla sherry

1 ounce / 30 ml celery juice

½ ounce / 15 ml Simple Syrup (see Violet Fizz, page 22)

½ ounce / 15 ml freshly squeezed lemon juice

Pinch kosher salt

Gose to top, about 3 ounces / 90 ml

Garnish: Celery stick, sea salt

Combine the sherry, celery juice, syrup, lemon juice, and salt in a cocktail shaker with ice and vigorously shake. Strain into a tall glass over ice and top with the gose. Gently stir just to incorporate, garnish, and serve.

SILVER COMPASS

Elderflowers bloom at the end of Spring, their clusters of star-shaped blossoms opening like ivory parasols with tiny yellow antennae. Their fragrance is intoxicating IRL and in the Silver Compass, a cocktail that keeps you thinking. It's got the honeyed musk of elderflower liqueur, the agave heat of tequila, the peaty smoke of Scotch, and the brightness of lemon all woven together into a strange, subtle, and wonderful springtime drink. Foragers and wildcrafters, this is a great place to feature your homemade elderflower syrup—simply substitute that for the agave nectar and omit the liqueur.

MAKES 1 COCKTAIL

¼ ounce / 7 ml Scotch

2 ounces / 60 ml blanco tequila

½ ounce / 15 ml elderflower liqueur

½ ounce / 15 ml freshly squeezed lemon juice

½ ounce / 15 ml light agave nectar

Rinse a short glass with the Scotch: Add and slowly rotate the Scotch around the inside of the glass to coat it completely. Combine the remaining ingredients in a mixing glass with ice and briskly stir. Strain the cocktail into the Scotch-rinsed glass, add fresh ice, and serve.

HAWTHORNE

Think of the Hawthorne as the *Backcountry Cocktails* martini, on the rocks. And like that classic, it's stiff and icy and best savored in the magic limbo between work and dinner. Work in this case could mean actual work or any number of strenuous outdoor endeavors: splitting a cord of firewood or a particularly arduous hike. Whatever the activity, you deserve a comfortable seat on a porch, cliff, or riverbank and a large glass of this. The Hawthorne itself is based on a 1925 cocktail fittingly called Spring. Though it's not especially springy, we ran with the original trio of gin (bracing), Dubonnet (aromatic and bitter), and Bénédictine (spiced and sweet) and pulled in orange blossom water, which speaks in a floral whisper, and a chunky olive-and-lemon garnish that gives big aperitivo vibes. We like to serve the Hawthorne over a single large ice rock or sphere, but if you didn't travel with your silicone molds, don't worry; this cocktail is just as effective over plain cubes.

MAKES 1 COCKTAIL

2 ounces / 60 ml gin

½ ounce / 15 ml Dubonnet Rouge

½ ounce / 15 ml Bénédictine

6 drops orange blossom water

Garnish: Speared green olives and lemon peel

Combine the gin, Dubonnet, Bénédictine, and orange blossom water in a mixing glass with ice and briskly stir. Strain into a short glass over a large single cube, garnish, and serve.

How to:
SCARE A BEAR

BY ERIC MORRIS

Before you go into the woods, know which animals live in those woods. That starts with utilizing resources like the local game warden, who can give you a download on deadly fauna, whether they're mountain lions, coyotes, snakes, or, yes, bears. That said, even the best-prepared hiker can have an unexpected run-in with a potentially dangerous creature—a bear, in this case. First, the good news: Unless your ursine encounter occurs in the relatively small grizzly territory (from Alaska down to Colorado through Washington, Montana, Idaho, and Wyoming), you're very likely facing a black bear. And while they are still large, powerful animals, black bears by nature are shy and nonconfrontational unless threatened. Should you meet one on a hike, here's what to do.

1. Don't panic. Remember that black bears are not typically violent or aggressive.

2. Assess your environment. At 60 to 100 yards from the bear, you have a good chance of avoiding confrontation. The closer you are, the fewer options you have. Bears can cover shorter distances quickly.

3. Do not run, which may spark a predatory reaction in the bear.

4. Slowly begin backing away while making loud noises. As a rule, you should be making plenty of noise (talking, singing, wearing a bell around your neck) while hiking in the wild, especially off-trail, to let bears know you're in the vicinity. They don't want unexpected guests any more than you do.

5. If the bear doesn't depart the area and begins to approach, you need to deter it from coming closer. Discharge bear spray according to the manufacturer's directions.

6. If these steps are followed, the likelihood that the bear will turn and leave is very high. Once the scene is clear, you can continue on or abandon your hike, depending how the close encounter has left you feeling.

HEMENWAY DAIQUIRI

Pine cones start out looking very different from the dried holiday ornaments they often wind up as. In Spring, they're tight green cocoons covered in pebbles or scales, and they taste distinctly of the forest. Italians steep them in sugar syrup to create mugolio, which is thick, sweet, tangy, and the darkest shade of brown before black. Mugolio brings a woodsy echo to our Hemenway Daiquiri, which is named for the 2,100-acre state forest in New Hampshire that is home to the Big Pines Natural Area. You can make your own by macerating unripe foraged cones with sugar for about two months, then boiling and straining that into a syrup, though it's much easier to buy Primitivizia's excellent mugolio from the Dolomite Alps online.

MAKES 1 COCKTAIL

2 ounces / 60 ml white rum

¾ ounce / 22 ml freshly squeezed lime juice

¾ ounce / 22 ml mugolio (pine cone syrup)

Garnish: Expressed lime peel

Combine the rum, lime juice, and mugolio in a shaker with ice, vigorously shake, and strain the cocktail into a chilled coupe. Garnish and serve.

EXPRESSED WHAT?

When you see us call for an expressed peel in any of the recipes, it just means you're releasing the essential oils from the citrus onto and into the drink. To express a peel, hold the peel zest down and squeeze it between your fingers over the surface of the drink. Then run the peel around the rim of the glass and drop it into the drink.

CHAMOMILE RHUBARB SPRITZ

Rhubarb is one of the earliest crops to force itself up out of the thawed spring soil, its leggy pink-and-chartreuse stems destined for pies and preserves . . . and shrubs, when we have our way. A shrub is an old-fashioned refresher made from blending fruit or vegetable syrup with vinegar and water, and our tongue-twistingly tangy rhubarb version, scented with fellow springtime arrival chamomile, brings out a wild side in this otherwise standard, well-mannered spritz.

The recipe for the shrub concentrate makes more than you need for the spritz. Fortunately, it's just as delicious and thirst-quenching when added to still or sparkling water. Start with a ratio of one part concentrate to six parts water of choice, then taste and add more concentrate until you reach your preferred strength of flavor. And a note on chamomile: Use fresh if you can find it. It grows like a weed in many places, and the plant's musky honey aroma is greener and more nuanced than the dried buds. Chamomile tea, however, works in a pinch.

MAKES 1 COCKTAIL

3 ounces / 90 ml sparkling white wine

2 ounces / 60 ml Campari

1 ounce / 30 ml seltzer

¾ ounce / 22 ml Chamomile Rhubarb Shrub Concentrate

Garnish: Chamomile blossoms

Combine the wine, Campari, seltzer, and Chamomile Rhubarb Shrub Concentrate in a wine glass with ice and briskly stir to combine. Garnish and serve.

CHAMOMILE RHUBARB SHRUB CONCENTRATE

MAKES ABOUT 2½ CUPS / 600 ML

2 rhubarb stalks, peeled and roughly chopped

1 cup / 200 g granulated sugar

½ cup / 50 g fresh chamomile blossoms (or substitute 1 chamomile teabag)

1 cup / 250 ml Champagne vinegar or white wine vinegar

Combine the rhubarb and the sugar in a large glass or plastic quart jar or other sturdy container. Close the container and shake so the sugar evenly coats the rhubarb. Allow the mixture to macerate at room temperature for 2 days, shaking once a day. During this time, the juices of the rhubarb will combine with the sugar to make a syrup. Add the chamomile and allow the mixture to rest another day. Strain off and reserve the syrup, pressing as much liquid out of the solids as possible. Combine the syrup and vinegar in a new container and store in the refrigerator, where it will keep for 2 weeks.

LOST RIVER MOSQUITO

The four-mile Lost River, one of New Hampshire's natural wonders, disappears into a glacial gorge, flowing underground and emerging in waterfalls along granite boulders. The Lost River Mosquito disappears, as well, on warm spring days that call for a refreshing, herbaceous cocktail. Like a Forager's Smash (page 13), this is a muddled drink, created by crushing cooling cucumbers and lemon in pisco, the clear Peruvian brandy, and stirring them together with aromatic bay-leaf syrup and butterfly pea flower tea, which shifts from deep indigo to purple as it encounters the acid in the lemon.

MAKES 1 COCKTAIL

2 ounces / 60 ml pisco

2 cucumber wheels

2 lemon slices

½ ounce / 15 ml Bay Syrup

4 ounces / 120 ml brewed and chilled butterfly pea flower tea

Garnish: Cucumber wheel, bay leaf

Gently muddle the pisco, cucumber, and lemon in the bottom of a short glass. Add the syrup, stir to combine, and then fill the glass with ice. Top with the butterfly pea tea, gently stir, garnish, and serve.

BAY SYRUP
MAKES 1 CUP / 240 ML

8 fresh bay leaves

¾ cup / 180 ml water

¾ cup / 150 g granulated sugar

Place the bay leaves and water in a small pot on the stove, grill, or campfire and bring it to a boil. Remove from the heat, cover the pot, and allow the bay leaves to steep for 5 minutes. Add the sugar and whisk to completely dissolve. Cover the pot and allow the syrup to cool for 30 minutes. Strain out the bay leaves, transfer the syrup to a jar, and store cold until ready to use.

HONEYSUCKLE PUNCH

"The scent of honeysuckle hangs in the darkness like the thick glop of sugar at the bottom of a glass of lemonade," novelist Erika Robuck writes in her book *Call Me Zelda*, and we're quoting her at the top of this punch recipe because a finer description for the intoxicating character of this plant eludes us. Here in New Hampshire, rambling walls of wild honeysuckle suddenly pop late in the Spring, with thousands of spidery ivory and butter-colored blossoms appearing against a background of dark green. They vanish as abruptly as they arrive, so collect as many as you can for as long as you can, preserving this fleeting time in Honeysuckle Syrup. Unlike other syrup recipes, this one is cold-infused, as the delicate blossoms will wilt into a swampy, unpleasant mess if they sit for long in hot liquid. After infusing overnight, you'll have an elixir that's nectary, libidinous, and borderline unbearably fragrant. Better angels might recommend enjoying it in measured doses, like an exorbitant perfume or super-dark chocolate bar. You won't find those angels here. We'll tell you that life is short and you should blow the whole batch on fizzy Honeysuckle Punch, an exuberant send-off for the year's micro-est of microseasons.

MAKES 6 TO 8 COCKTAILS

2 cups / 480 ml cachaça

1 cup / 240 ml bianco vermouth

1 cup / 240 ml Honeysuckle Syrup

¾ cup / 180 ml freshly squeezed lemon juice

1 (12 ounce / 355 ml) can passion fruit LaCroix sparkling water (apricot, watermelon, and grapefruit also work well)

Garnish: Lemon wheels

Combine the cachaça, vermouth, syrup, and lemon juice in a large pitcher or serving bowl. Stir and then chill the mixture for at least 1 hour and up to a day. Add the sparkling water right before serving, stir, garnish, and serve.

HONEYSUCKLE SYRUP

MAKES 1 CUP / 240 ML

¾ cup / 180 ml water

¾ cup / 150 g granulated sugar

½ cup (loosely packed) / 50 g honeysuckle blossoms, gently washed

Place the water in a small pot on the stove, grill, or campfire and bring it to a boil. Remove it from the heat, add the sugar, and whisk to completely dissolve. Allow the syrup to cool to room temperature. Add the honeysuckle to a glass jar and pour the cooled syrup over it. Close the jar and allow the mixture to cold-infuse overnight in the fridge or a well-chilled cooler. Strain out the honeysuckle, return the finished syrup to the jar, and store cold until ready to use.

How to:
FERMENT VEGGIES

BY JAMAAR JULAL

Lactic acid bacteria (LAB), also known as Lactobacillales, are microorganisms found on all plants. While they only make up roughly 1 percent of a given plant's microbial population, they're the driving force behind lacto-fermentation, one of the simpler ferments to handle and among the most common. This process is responsible for kitchen staples like pickles, sauerkraut, kimchi, and even yogurt and cheese when given the appropriate push. In the right environment, LAB can multiply and flourish from that 1 percent, preserving produce in the process by inhibiting the growth of other microorganisms that contribute to spoilage while also imparting a new complexity of flavor. This environment is salty and anaerobic (without oxygen), and the most straightforward way to create it is through a brine. Since it's Spring, we're using ramps to illustrate this guide, but the process is essentially the same for all vegetables—though you'll want a saltier brine for cucumbers and other produce that gets mushy during fermentation.

1. Very gently rinse about ½ pound / 200 g ramps under cold water to remove any excess dirt. Emphasis on "gentle"; the leaves are covered in LAB that we want to keep around for the fermentation process.

2. Wrap each ramp horizontally around the inside of a cleaned and sterilized, wide-mouth, 32-ounce / 1-L glass jar. Pack them well but not too tightly, working toward the center of the jar, until it is three-quarters full.

3. When lacto-fermenting, you want a brine that is 2 to 5 percent salt. For ramps, cabbages, and leafy greens, 3 percent makes a solid brine. Combine 2 cups plus 2 tablespoons / 500 ml cold, filtered water with a scant tablespoon / 15 g Diamond Crystal or 1 ½ scant teaspoons Morton or kosher salt. (Fifteen grams is 3 percent of 500 g—math!) Allow the salt to dissolve in the water.

4. Pour enough brine over the ramps to completely cover them. The ramps may float when the brine is added. If that happens, weigh them down with a glass, ceramic, or stoneware weight; they should remain submerged below the brine at all times.

5. At this point you can add any aromatics you like. A mix well suited to ramps is 1 dried chile de árbol, ½ teaspoon wild garlic mustard seed, ½ teaspoon herbes de Provence, and 2 cardamom pods. This is the most exciting part of fermentation, because there are no limitations on trying different combinations of flavors.

6. Close the jar and allow the ramps to ferment at room temperature (70 to 75°F / 21 to 24°C) for 3 days. After the third day, burp the jar by opening the lid to release the CO_2 that will have built up as the LAB breaks down carbohydrates. Signs of a healthy ferment include bubbles and the brine becoming cloudy.

7. Continue to ferment for 4 additional days, burping the jar and tasting the ramps once daily. The longer they ferment, the stronger the flavor will become, so it's very much up to your preference when to cut off the process by transferring the jar to the fridge.

CRISPY CAST-IRON TROUT WITH WILD GREENS

Whether you caught the fish or bought the fish, here's a low-maintenance, delicious dinner for two that comes together in about 10 minutes and requires nothing but a sturdy cast-iron pan and a spoon. You can make it in all seasons, but it's particularly good in Spring, when all the wild greens are cropping up.

MAKES 2 SERVINGS

2 tablespoons vegetable oil

2 skin-on trout filets, 6 to 8 ounces / 175 to 250 g each

Kosher salt and black pepper, to taste

2 tablespoons salted butter

1 tablespoon capers

Juice of ½ lemon

4 cups torn mixed wild greens, such as dandelion, mustard, sorrel, and ramp tops

Garnish: Chopped parsley

Preheat a large cast-iron skillet over medium heat over a campfire, grill, or stove for 5 minutes. Add the oil to the pan and season the trout on both sides with salt and pepper. Carefully add the trout, skin side down, and allow it to cook undisturbed until the skin is crispy, about 6 minutes. Add the butter and capers. Spoon the butter over the flesh side of the fish as it melts. Add the lemon and greens and cook until the greens are just beginning to wilt. Season with salt and pepper, plate, garnish, and serve.

ORANGE TARRAGON FREEZE

Sometimes you barely have enough energy to crack open a beer, let alone mix a cocktail, after a long day hiking in the ferocious summer heat. But with a little advance planning you can toast the sunset with this citrusy herbal sparkler. Here's how it works: You prepare and freeze the cocktail overnight right in a water bottle, stash it in your pack in the morning, and after several hours of hiking (five to eight, depending on the ambient temperature—listen for the ice cubes clunking around), the Orange Tarragon Freeze will be, well, unfrozen and ready to drink. And because CO_2 holds a bubble best in cold liquids, it maintains its effervescence. This recipe is also super adaptable. While we love how sweet orange and anise-y tarragon get along, you can slide in any citrus and herb you like. Grapefruit-basil and lemon-rosemary are two combos we heartily endorse.

MAKES 2 COCKTAILS

4 ounces / 120 ml vodka

4 ounces / 120 ml freshly squeezed orange juice

2 ounces / 60 ml triple sec

2 ounces / 60 ml Tarragon Syrup

16 ounces / 450 g ice cubes

4 ounces / 120 ml seltzer

Add the vodka, orange juice, triple sec, syrup, and ice cubes to a 32-ounce / 1-L plastic water bottle, seal, and gently shake. Add the seltzer, tightly seal the bottle, and gently rotate it to integrate the cocktail without exciting too much carbonation. Slightly loosen the lid, which will allow air to escape when the contents of the bottle expand while freezing, and place the bottle upright in the freezer overnight. In the morning, seal the lid tightly and store the bottle in your pack—the hotter the outside temperature, the deeper you should store it in your pack—until thawed and ready to drink.

TARRAGON SYRUP

MAKES 1 CUP / 240 ML

½ cup / 14 g (loosely packed) tarragon leaves

¾ cup / 180 ml water

¾ cup / 150 g granulated sugar

Place the tarragon and the water in a small pot on the stove, grill, or campfire and bring it to a boil. Remove it from the heat, cover the pot, and allow the tarragon to steep for 5 minutes. Add the sugar and whisk to completely dissolve. Cover the pot and allow the syrup to cool for 30 minutes. Strain out the tarragon, transfer the syrup to a jar, and store cold until ready to use.

PISCATAQUA MICHELADA

When you're enveloped in the White Mountains, it's hard to conceive that the ocean is only about 70 miles due east. That drive brings you down through the dense evergreen forest, through thinning woods and across a network of marshes, rivers, and bays that have supported clamming and oystering for centuries. Garnished with seafood skewers, our version of the heat-busting michelada nods to the seafood harvesting heritage of New Hampshire and Maine, and the Piscataqua River that divides them. You'll be sourcing tinned seafood for this recipe, which is fully cooked and a breeze to pack. Legacy outfits from Spain and Portugal, where conserving seafood is an ancient art, are no-brainers, but North American companies like Alaska's Wildfish Cannery and Prince Edward Island's Scout also produce high-quality products. Our move is to mix and match: smoked oysters, brined razor clams, marinated mussels, olive-oiled cockles, interspersed with bright green olives. Assemble them in advance if you're short on space or on the move, or if you have a picnic table or catamaran deck to work with, set out a whole tinned seafood extravaganza and let people create their own skewers.

MAKES 1 COCKTAIL

4 ounces / 120 ml Clamato juice

½ ounce / 15 ml freshly squeezed lemon juice

3 dashes Worcestershire sauce

1 tablespoon prepared cocktail sauce

Hot sauce, to taste

4 ounces / 120 ml light lager

Garnish: Skewered olive, tinned seafood of choice, and lemon wedge

Stir the Clamato, lemon juice, Worcestershire sauce, cocktail sauce, and hot sauce together in a tall glass. Fill the glass with ice, then slowly pour in the beer. Gently stir the michelada to incorporate, garnish with the skewer, and serve.

Take It to Go: Scale up the michelada mix by six, pour it back into the empty Clamato bottle, and pack it with a sixer of beer.

XMAS IN JULY

Half nightcap, half dessert, this spiced vanilla-and-fig-flavored dream is a perfect way to wind down a long summer day. We can see your raised eyebrow: *Ice cream and preserves?* But we promise, it's not too sweet. Xmas in July is a whiskey drink through and through—so good that you'll make it in June and August, too.

MAKES 1 COCKTAIL

2 ounces / 60 ml bourbon

1 tablespoon fig preserves

4 dashes chai spice bitters

4 ounces / 120 ml vanilla ice cream (about 1 scoop)

Garnish: Grated cinnamon

Combine the bourbon, preserves, bitters, and ice cream in a cocktail shaker with a single ice cube and vigorously shake until the ice is melted and the ingredients sound uniform and foamy inside. Pour the cocktail into a short glass over ice. Garnish and serve.

How to:
PACK A COOLER

BY LEE NOBLE

To successfully camp in the Summer is to be a truce broker, continually finessing an armistice between archnemeses: your food (and drink) and the heat. A properly packed cooler is your first line of defense, and it begins before you even put one item inside. If you store your cooler in a warm place like an attic or garage, bring it into the kitchen the day before your trip so it gets cool. This will help you avoid packing ice and ingredients into a warm cooler, which could compromise the ice and food quality. Even better is to chill the cooler an hour prior to packing: Put some ice in the cooler, close the lid tightly, and wait. Then follow the steps below to ensure your bacon and grapes and s'mores provisions stay cool no matter the temperature outside.

1. Line the bottom of a large cooler with fresh ice. (Anywhere we mention ice in this guide, you can substitute cooler packs.)

2. Place any meats in watertight bags or containers to avoid cross contamination and arrange them in an even layer on top of the ice.

3. Place any perishable fruits and vegetables in watertight bags or containers and arrange them on top of the meats. Durable produce (broccoli, eggplant) should go in first, followed by delicate items like tomatoes and peaches.

4. Gently pack ice into any empty space between foods to eliminate warm air pockets. Cover the produce with an even layer of ice, leaving enough room to pack the final category: snacks.

5. Any drinks or snacks you want handy during the car ride or upon immediate arrival at camp are the last things to be packed. Add them above the top layer of ice. (Other drinks, including cocktail supplies that require chilling, should be packed in a second cooler, ideally a travel-sized one you can easily transport to a boat, fishing hole, etc.)

6. Shut the cooler tightly and keep it out of the sun at all times.

HIBISCUS PALOMA

Don't tell the margarita, but the paloma is actually the greatest tequila cocktail. This two-part thirst-quencher involves blanco tequila (aka silver) and grapefruit soda, either homemade with juice, sweetener, and seltzer or off the shelf courtesy of a bottle of Squirt or Jarritos Toronja. This version weaves in the refreshing cranberry flavor—and striking fuchsia color—of hibiscus with a simple overnight infusion. This is a batched recipe that makes four cocktails. Share or keep them all to yourself and consume over a couple days. Without seltzer, which gets added right before serving, the batch will keep in the fridge or cooler for a week.

MAKES 4 COCKTAILS

1 cup / 250 ml silver tequila

4 ounces / 120 ml freshly squeezed grapefruit juice

2 ounces / 60 ml freshly squeezed lime juice

2 ounces / 60 ml light agave nectar

½ ounce / 14 g dried hibiscus flowers

Seltzer

Garnish: Lime wheels

Combine the tequila, grapefruit juice, lime juice, agave nectar, and hibiscus flowers in a glass or plastic quart jar or other sturdy container and refrigerate overnight. Strain out the hibiscus flowers in the morning, return the mixture to the container, and pack it in a cooler. When ready to serve, gently shake and pour a quarter of the mixture into a tall glass filled with ice. (Or evenly divide it between 4 glasses.) Top with seltzer, garnish, and serve.

BLACKBERRY BASIL SOUR

Ripe blackberries and fragrant basil go—and grow—together. This cocktail is a straightforward adaptation of the whiskey sour, with the berries and herb muddled first to release the former's violet nectar and the latter's essential oils for a fruity, aromatic summer drink that looks as alluring as it tastes.

MAKES 1 COCKTAIL

6 large basil leaves

4 blackberries

¾ ounce / 22 ml freshly squeezed lemon juice

2 ounces / 60 ml rye whiskey

White from 1 large egg or 1 ounce / 30 ml aquafaba

¾ ounce / 22 ml crème de cassis, Chambord, or other dark berry liqueur

Garnish: Skewered blackberries, basil sprig

Thoroughly muddle the basil and berries in the lemon juice in the bottom of a cocktail shaker.

Add the whiskey, egg white, and crème de cassis and vigorously shake to whip the egg white. Add ice, vigorously shake again, and strain over fresh ice into a short glass. Garnish and serve.

WHITE PORT PEACH COBBLER

A pre-Prohibition gem, the cobbler brings together fortified wine, citrus, sugar, crushed (FKA "cobbled") ice, and a garnishing jungle of fruit and herbs. Tailored for Summer, this day-drinking companion eschews sugar for the natural sweetness in ripe peaches and white port, and looks to lemon for brightness and balance. It seems sophisticated but is so easygoing, not to mention low-ABV.

MAKES 1 COCKTAIL

2 peach slices

2 ounces / 60 ml white port

½ ounce / 15 ml freshly squeezed lemon juice

Garnish: Peach slice, lemon wheel, mint sprig, straw

Gently muddle the peaches and port in the bottom of a tall glass. Add the lemon juice, fill the glass with crushed ice, and briskly stir to combine. Top up with more ice as needed, garnish, and serve.

How to:
PRESERVE FRUIT

Making jam is one of the oldest fruit preservation methods—an easy way to extend the life of a bountiful harvest from a farm, the woods, or even the grocery store. The guide below is a basic template that will work with any summer fruit, with two caveats: Since every berry and fig and plum is different, you may need to tweak the sugar and acid up or down to achieve a balance that feels right for your tastes. And fruit that gives off a ton of liquid, like blueberries, may require the assistance of powdered pectin to tighten things up to the proper consistency.

1. Combine 2 pounds / 1 kg (about 6 cups) fruit of choice, 2 cups / 400 g granulated sugar, 1 teaspoon Diamond Crystal (or ½ teaspoon Morton) kosher salt, ¼ cup / 60 ml freshly squeezed lemon juice, and spices or flavorings of choice in a medium Dutch oven or other heavy-bottomed pot.

2. Bring the mixture to a boil over medium-high heat and allow it to boil, stirring frequently, for 15 minutes. Reduce the heat to medium-low and continue to stir until most of the liquid has evaporated and the preserves are thick and jammy, 45 minutes to 1 hour.

3. Thoroughly clean and sanitize two to four 8-ounce / 250-ml glass canning jars and their lids.

4. Fill the jars with the jam, leaving about 1 inch / 2.5 cm of headspace. Remove air bubbles by gently tapping the jars on the counter and/or running a cleaned and sterilized knife around the edges. Screw on the lids.

5. Using a jar lifter, carefully lower the jars of jam into a large pot of boiling water so they are fully submerged. Boil for 9 minutes.

6. Using a jar lifter, carefully remove the jars and place them on a kitchen towel. Allow them to cool undisturbed; as they come down to room temperature, the lids will create an airtight seal and become slightly concave. When the jars are cool enough to handle, test the seal by pressing the middle of the lid; if it springs up when you release your finger, the jar did not seal, and the jam inside must be stored in the fridge and used within 2 weeks. Successfully sealed jam can be stored at room temperature for up to a year.

BOURBON PEACH HAND PIES

Now that you're jamming along like a 17th-century survivalist, it's time to put those preserves to work inside homemade hand pies. Unlike a fresh fruit pie, these quick-baking, tidy, portable pastries are ideally suited to jam. Make a batch the night before a trip, pack them in the morning, and you'll have breakfast, a snack, or dessert standing by. For the jam filling, this recipe spikes classic peach with bourbon, but feel free to use whatever preserves are burning a hole in your cabin cupboard.

MAKES 4 SERVINGS

2 lemons

2 pounds / 1 kg pitted sliced peaches

2 cups / 400 g granulated sugar

1 teaspoon Diamond Crystal
(or ½ teaspoon Morton) kosher salt

¼ cup / 60 ml bourbon

1 teaspoon vanilla extract

1 piece fresh ginger, about
2 inches / 5 cm, grated

All-purpose flour, for dusting

2 prepared 9-inch / 23-cm
pie crusts

1 large egg, beaten

Granulated sugar, for dusting

Juice and zest the lemons and reserve. Prepare the peach jam through step 2 of the instructions in How to: Preserve Fruit (page 68) with ¼ cup / 60 ml of the reserved lemon juice, the peaches, sugar, salt, bourbon, vanilla, and ginger. When the jam has completely cooled, stir in the lemon zest.

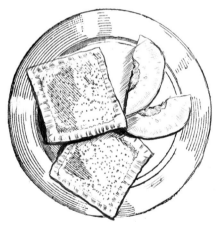

   Preheat the oven to 350°F / 175°C and line a sheet pan with parchment paper. Lightly flour a cutting board and unroll one pie crust. Press it out with a rolling pin, then trim with a pizza cutter or knife to create a roughly square shape. Cut the square down the middle to create 2 rectangles, which will be folded over to make 2 tarts. Spread about ¼ cup / 60 ml of jam on the lower half of each rectangle, leaving a ½-inch / 1.3-cm border around the edges. Gently fold the upper half of each rectangle toward you and over the jam so it meets the opposite end. Crimp the tarts on all sides with a fork, then carefully transfer to the prepared pan. Repeat this process for the second pie crust, creating 4 tarts total.

Brush the tarts with the egg and lightly dust sugar over the surface. Bake them for 30 minutes or until golden brown. Cool at least 10 minutes before eating and cool completely before packing in foil or sandwich bags.

BARK AND STORMY

Strappy silver birches brighten forests all over New England, and just like maples, the state tree of New Hampshire can be tapped for the sweet sap trapped inside. Birch syrup tastes like maple crossed with molasses and laced with whispers of wintergreen and pine. It's curious and completely bewitching, both in cooking and in cocktails like the Bark and Stormy. Unlike its inspiration, the Caribbean classic dark and stormy, our New England version uses birch beer instead of ginger beer. Birch syrup can be a little hard to track down (though the Gateway Farm in Bristol, Vermont, ships nationwide), but this easy pour-and-stir cocktail is also perfectly delicious with bottled soda. Squamscot, the legacy New Hampshire sodaworks, makes a terrific birch beer.

MAKES 1 COCKTAIL

1½ ounces / 45 ml rum añejo

½ ounce / 15 ml birch syrup

4 dashes molasses bitters

Seltzer to top, 2 to 4 ounces / 60 to 120 ml

Garnish: Lemon wedge, mint sprig

Fill a short glass with ice. Add the rum, syrup, and bitters and stir. Top with seltzer and stir, garnish, and serve. If you don't have birch syrup, omit the syrup and substitute birch beer for the seltzer.

LAVENDER MINT LOJITO

Sweet mint and floral lavender: the perfumed power couple of the summer meadow. Fresh leaves of the former and a lilac syrup made from the buds of the latter rendezvous in this low-ABV twist on the mojito. Replacing the rum (80 proof) with the aromatized wine Lillet (34 proof) brings the alcohol content way, way down—a smart move for sweltering summer days spent outdoors—but also introduces a whole bonus bouquet of herbal notes to create a mojito that's complex *and* refreshing.

MAKES 1 COCKTAIL

6 mint leaves

½ small lime, quartered

1½ ounces / 45 ml Lillet Blanc

¾ ounce / 22 ml Lavender Syrup

Seltzer to top, 2 to 4 ounces / 60 to 120 ml

Garnish: Lavender and mint sprigs, lime wheel

Vigorously muddle the mint and lime with the Lillet in the bottom of a tall glass. Add the lavender syrup and ice and stir. Top with seltzer and stir. Garnish and serve.

LAVENDER SYRUP
MAKES 1 CUP / 240 ML

¼ cup / 25 g dried lavender flowers

¾ cup / 180 ml water

¾ cup / 150 g granulated sugar

Place the lavender and water in a small pot on the stove, grill, or campfire and bring to a boil. Remove from the heat, cover, and allow the lavender to steep for 5 minutes. Strain out and discard the flowers, return the syrup to the pot, and add the sugar. Whisk until the sugar is completely dissolved and allow the syrup to come to room temperature. Transfer it to a glass or plastic pint jar or other sturdy container and store cold until ready to use.

BACKCOUNTRY COLD BREW

The long and honorable tradition of spiked coffee comes to the camp, with bottled cold brew and canned coconut milk that won't take up valuable cooler space. The medicinal slap of Fernet in the coconut-creamed coffee is pleasantly strange. You'll be scratching your head, then going back for a second cup.

MAKES 1 COCKTAIL

1 ounce / 30 ml Fernet-Branca

4 ounces / 120 ml cold-brewed coffee

1 ounce / 30 ml full-fat unsweetened coconut milk

½ ounce / 15 ml light agave nectar

Garnish: Grated cinnamon

Combine the fernet, coffee, coconut milk, and agave nectar in a cocktail shaker with ice and vigorously shake. Strain over fresh ice into a mug, garnish, and serve.

Take It to Go: Triple the recipe and load into an insulated travel cup or water bottle. Chill overnight and sip while you hike or kayak.

AMERI-CAN-O

Hard seltzers have become as inescapable during Summer as tan lines and mosquito bites. You can resist them, but sooner or later, they'll find you. Credit where credit is due: Some breweries and distilleries produce pretty palatable versions, and on a steamy day, hard seltzers can be convenient and refreshing. So here's a fizzy cocktail you make right in the can. Crack, swig, add sweet vermouth, Aperol, an orange twist, and *voilà!* You've essentially created a portable Americano, the lower-proof negroni ancestor of sweet vermouth, Campari, and seltzer— except the seltzer in question is alcoholic and perhaps strawberry-kiwi flavored. We call it the Ameri-can-o: a little Lake Como, a little Lake of the Ozarks, a lot of fun. Use whatever brand and flavor you like, though cherry, berry, and citrus seltzers work particularly well.

MAKES 1 COCKTAIL

1 can hard seltzer of choice, chilled

½ ounce / 15 ml sweet vermouth, chilled

½ ounce / 15 ml Aperol, chilled

Garnish: Orange peel, straw

Crack the can of seltzer and take a big sip. Add the vermouth and Aperol, tuck the orange peel into the can, add the straw, and serve.

Take It to Go: For a sixer of seltzers, combine 3 ounces / 90 ml each of the vermouth and Aperol in a glass or plastic pint jar or other sturdy container. Store cold until ready to use.

SUGAR · 100 CALORIES · GLUTEN FREE · NO ADD

HIGH NOON

SUN SIPS™

VODKA & SODA

BLACK CHERRY
MADE WITH REAL JUICE

VODKA WITH REAL FRUIT JUICE,
SPARKLING WATER & NATURAL FLAVORS

4.5% ALC. BY VOL. | 355 mL

GLEN ELLIS FALLS TRAIL
GLEN ELLIS FALLS 0.3 ↑
WILDCAT RIDGE TRAIL ↑
(THROUGH UNDERPASS)

GLEN BOULDER TRAIL →

BY LEE NOBLE

A well-constructed and secured tent is a camper's protection against the elements and pests. These instructions assume you're camping in a designated site, like those at national parks or forests. If you're way off trail, prepare to hike to a clearing or create your own—but honestly, if you're that deep in the backwoods and need this guide to tell you how to set up camp, we've got bigger problems to talk about.

1. Identify the designated tent pads in your campsite. They are typically flat, level areas, about 10 feet / 3 m square, away from the fire pit, and they are generally clear of ground cover, brush, and protruding roots and rocks. Be sure to look above the tent pads before pitching your tent, in case there are any precarious branches (called widow makers) hanging from the trees above. In that case, you should notify the camp manager or any available park or forest service personnel about the risk and find another pad for the tent.

2. Sweep the tent pad of any debris. You can do this with your hands or a dead-and-downed tree branch, often found around campsites, as a broom.

3. Unpack the tent, poles, stakes, rain fly, and guy lines, and lay them out in an organized manner. Depending on the weather and style of tent, you may benefit from placing a durable plastic tarp under the tent to protect the tent from wear and possible water infiltration.

4. Follow the directions for putting up the tent, including the tarp underneath and the rain fly to cover the tent, as needed. This can differ depending on make, model, style, and so on, and is often as simple as laying the tent out upright and flat, and then running long poles through hooks and grommets in the roof of the tent in order to get it to stand up, and then securing them tightly. Make sure the entrance faces in the desired direction (some people like to wake up and stumble right into the woods to answer nature's call, and others like to step out of their tent to the best view from the campsite).

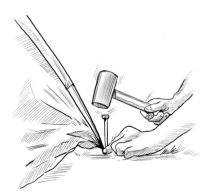

5. Stake the tent down tightly in case of any wind. In case of extreme wind, guy lines, the supportive ropes that can be lashed to the outside of the tent and staked into the ground, may be necessary. Follow the manufacturer's directions for use.

6. Be sure the tent is zipped closed tightly when not in use, to keep out pests and wildlife.

GRILLED CORN, CLAM, AND PESTO PIZZA

Few aromas are as magnetizing as flames caressing pizza dough on a hot grill. It's that fresh-baked bread smell, tattooed with a toasty campfire char, then blended with the heady bouquet of high Summer in the mountains. Want to get everyone back to camp quickly? Grilled pizza is an olfactory dinner bell, not to mention dead simple to execute. This recipe uses prepared dough, so all you need to do is stretch and cook, which can be done either on a gas or charcoal grill or over a live campfire. Sweet summer corn, pesto, clams—a New England thing—and smoked mozzarella go beautifully together, but you can freestyle whatever topping you like.

MAKES 6 SERVINGS

Extra-virgin olive oil, for brushing and drizzling

1 pound / 454 g prepared pizza dough, at room temperature

¾ cup / 191 g prepared pesto

6 ounces / 170 g smoked mozzarella, shredded

½ cup / 75 g fresh corn kernels

6 to 8 ounces / 170 to 226 g fresh or canned cooked clams, shucked and drained

Large basil leaves, for serving

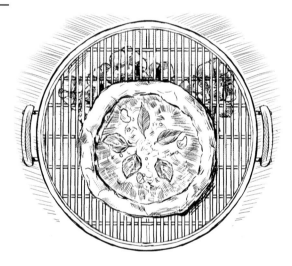

GAS OR CHARCOAL GRILL: Set up the grill with two zones—one high heat, the other low heat.

Carefully drape the dough across the hot grates, close the grill, and cook for 3 to 5 minutes, or until the dough begins to bubble and take on grill marks on the bottom. Carefully flip the dough over onto the low-heat side of the grill. Top the dough with the pesto, mozzarella, corn, and clams.

Close the grill and allow the pizza to finish cooking over low heat. Cook until the bottom takes on grill marks and the cheese has melted, about 3 minutes.

Remove the pizza from the grill, garnish with the basil, slice, and serve.

CAMPFIRE GRILL: Center a height-adjustable camping grill over the fire and adjust so it's about 3 inches / 8 cm above the flames or charcoal.

Brush the grates with the olive oil and allow them to preheat for 5 minutes, which will prevent the dough from sticking. While the grates heat, slowly stretch the pizza dough with cleaned and oiled hands until it's about 12 to 16 inches / 30 to 40 cm across.

Carefully drape the dough across the hot grates, cover with a dome, and cook for 3 to 5 minutes, or until the dough begins to bubble and take on grill marks on the bottom. Carefully flip the dough over and raise the grill so it's clear of the heat.

Lower the grill to 6 inches / 15 cm above the fire and cover the pizza with a dome to finish cooking. Cook until the bottom takes on grill marks and the cheese has melted, about 3 minutes.

Remove the pizza from the grill, garnish with the basil, slice, and serve.

WHITE MOUNTAIN WATERMELON SANGRIA

Three reasons sangria is an unexpectedly perfect wilderness beverage: (1) You can make it in advance. (2) Like cherry pie and clam chowder, it's even better the next day. (3) It feeds—or whatever the drink equivalent of *feeds* is—a crowd, making it ideal in the event you're camping, boating, or cabin-dwelling with friends or family. Sangria flotsam and jetsam can be anything you want, but this sweet and tangy trinity of watermelon, strawberries, and lime radiates Summer.

MAKES 10 TO 12 COCKTAILS

1 (750 ml) bottle pinot grigio or other dry white wine

1 cup / 250 ml brandy

½ cup / 125 ml freshly squeezed lime juice

1 lime, sliced into wheels

1½ cups / 228 g diced seedless watermelon

6 strawberries, hulled and quartered

1½ cups / 375 ml ginger beer

Combine the wine, brandy, lime juice, lime slices, watermelon, and strawberries in a large pitcher or serving bowl. Stir and chill the mixture for at least 1 hour and up to 1 day. Add the ginger beer right before serving, stir, and serve.

BLUE BEE G&T

Brisk, bittersweet, and botanical, the gin and tonic represents classic warm-weather refreshment, but what we really love about this drink is how riff-able it is. For such a straightforward cocktail, you can create endless versions by switching up the gin, the tonic, and the garnishes. The Blue Bee G&T is a forest jamboree of aromatic spruce tips, fat blueberries, and honey in three expressions, including a rare self-brag on Tamworth Garden Apiary Gin, made at our distillery in the White Mountains. Its honeyed evergreen character is absolutely made for this G&T, but if you can't find it, any piney gin will do.

MAKES 1 COCKTAIL

2 ounces / 60 ml Tamworth Garden Apiary Gin (or any other gin)

½ ounce / 15 ml Honey Syrup

¼ ounce / 7 ml freshly squeezed lemon juice

6 blueberries

2 lemon wheels

1 teaspoon bee pollen

3 spruce tips or rosemary sprigs

5 ounces / 150 ml tonic water

Combine all ingredients in a large glass over ice, briskly stir to combine, and serve.

HONEY SYRUP
MAKES 1 CUP / 240 ML

⅓ cup / 80 ml water

⅔ cup / 230 g honey

Bring the water to a boil in a small pot on the stove, grill, or campfire. Remove the pot from the heat, add the honey, and stir to completely dissolve. Allow the finished syrup to cool and transfer it to a glass or plastic pint jar or other sturdy container. Store cold until ready to use.

Autumn

SMOKY SAGE OLD FASHIONED

Woodsy sage, bittersweet grapefruit, and smoky mezcal tangle in this twist on the classic old fashioned. It's a thinker, straddling the line between warming and refreshing, which makes it ideal for those primo nights when Summer is giving way to Autumn. Enjoy it on the porch under a flannel blanket or at the end of a dock with your jeans rolled up and toes in the lake.

MAKES 1 COCKTAIL

2 ounces / 60 ml mezcal

½ ounce / 15 ml Sage Syrup

4 dashes grapefruit bitters

Garnish: Grapefruit slice, sage leaf

Combine the mezcal, syrup, and bitters in a short glass with ice and stir. Add more ice if needed, garnish, and serve.

SAGE SYRUP

MAKES 1 CUP / 240 ML

1 cup / 70 g (loosely packed) sage leaves

¾ cup / 180 ml water

¾ cup / 150 g granulated sugar

Place the sage and the water in a small pot on the stove, grill, or campfire and bring it to a boil. Remove from the heat, cover the pot, and allow the sage to steep for 5 minutes. Add the sugar and whisk to completely dissolve. Cover the pot and allow the syrup to cool for 30 minutes. Strain out the sage and transfer the finished syrup to a glass or plastic pint jar or other sturdy container. Store cold until ready to use.

MACK ROSE

"I was in the Hotel Crillon, waiting for Brett," says Jake Barnes, the narrator in Hemingway's *The Sun Also Rises*. Lady Brett Ashley, Jake's love interest, stands him up at the Paris hotel. "So about quarter to six I went down to the bar and had a Jack Rose with George the barman." The Jack Rose—applejack, lime, and grenadine served up—is an early-1900s classic and soother of bruised egos and broken hearts. Far away from France, we discovered a long-lost descendant of Jack's, Mack Rose, camped out in the White Mountains, where fuzzy burgundy claws of staghorn sumac clamber across the fields. This refresher highlights sumac in a sweet-and-tart syrup (replacing Jack's grenadine) and in a sugar rim. Fall is an ideal time to go foraging, but you can also buy high-quality dried and jarred sumac from companies like Burlap & Barrel and Frontier Co-op.

MAKES 1 COCKTAIL

Lemon wedge

Sumac Sugar

2 ounces / 60 ml applejack

1 ounce / 30 ml freshly squeezed lemon juice

½ ounce / 15 ml Sumac Syrup

3 dashes Peychaud's bitters

Garnish: Apple slice

Rub half of the rim of a chilled coupe glass with a lemon and dip it into the Sumac Sugar. Place the glass right side up. Combine the applejack, lemon juice, syrup, and bitters in a cocktail shaker with ice and vigorously shake. Strain the cocktail into the prepared glass, garnish, and serve.

SUMAC SYRUP

MAKES 1 CUP / 240 ML

1 tablespoon plus 1 teaspoon dried sumac

¾ cup / 180 ml water

¾ cup / 150 g granulated sugar

Place the sumac and the water in a small pot on the stove, grill, or campfire and bring it to a boil. Remove from the heat, cover the pot, and allow the sumac to steep for 5 minutes. Add the sugar and whisk to completely dissolve. Cover the pot and allow the syrup to cool for 30 minutes. Strain out the sumac and transfer the syrup to a glass or plastic pint jar or other sturdy container. Store cold until ready to use.

SUMAC SUGAR

MAKES 3 TABLESPOONS

2 tablespoons granulated sugar

1 tablespoon dried sumac

Combine the ingredients in a small jar or container, close, and gently shake to combine.

MULLED CAMPFIRE CIDER

Bourbon and cider go together like campfires and ghost stories, and sure, you could just throw the two together in a cup and be on your way to a cozy autumn evening. But taking the extra step to mull the cider with aromatic spices like cinnamon and clove makes all the difference. Hang a pot of that over your fire and within minutes the entire campsite smells like a holiday. What's nice about this recipe is that it works for all ages and all drinkers. For kids and those abstaining from alcohol for whatever reason, just skip the slug of bourbon. The mulled cider tastes delicious and feels special all on its own.

MAKES 4 COCKTAILS

1 quart / 1 L apple cider

2 oranges

8 cloves

2 cinnamon sticks

1 nutmeg, cracked

1 tablespoon chopped ginger

1 cup / 240 ml bourbon

Garnish: Clove-studded orange slices, cinnamon sticks

Bring the cider to a boil in a medium pot on the stove, grill, or campfire. Remove the peel from the oranges with a vegetable peeler, being careful to leave as much of the pith behind as possible. Twist them between your fingers to release the essential oils and add them to the cider. Gather the cloves, cinnamon sticks, nutmeg, and ginger in a cheesecloth pouch, tie it tightly, and add it to the cider. Cover the pot and simmer the cider for 30 minutes. Remove the orange peel and spice pouch and divide the mulled cider between 4 mugs. Add 2 ounces / 60 ml bourbon to each and stir. Garnish and serve.

Family Style: Add all the bourbon to the pot of mulled cider and stir. Float the orange slices on top and add a ladle for self-serving.

How to:
TRAVERSE A BEAVER DAM

BY LEE NOBLE

Nothing interrupts a leisurely canoe trip like a dam. Please mind the beavers.

1. Paddle the canoe up to the edge of the dam so the bow (front) touches it.

2. Have the bow paddler carefully step out of the canoe onto the dam, stepping on any sturdy branches and sticks so that they don't sink their leg into the dam. The bow paddler disembarking will shift the weight to the back of the boat, causing the front to pop out of the water.

3. Have the bow paddler grab the front and drag the canoe partway up onto the dam, far enough so the stern (rear) paddler can climb toward the front of the canoe in order to step out onto the dam. Have the bow paddler hold the canoe stable while the stern paddler climbs out.

4. Now that the weight of both paddlers is out of the canoe, it's safer to pull it across the dam the rest of the way without damaging the hull. Mind any sharp sticks sticking out of the dam and continue to watch where you step.

5. Once the front half of the canoe is back in the water on the other side of the dam, have the stern paddler hold the canoe still while the bow paddler climbs back in.

6. When the bow paddler is seated, have the stern paddler scoot the canoe the rest of the way into the water, holding on to the back gunwale to keep the canoe close.

7. With the stern paddler still standing on the dam and holding on to the back gunwale, have the bow paddler paddle gently so the front of the canoe comes toward the dam, until the entire canoe is parked parallel to the dam. This makes it easier for the stern paddler to get back into the canoe.

8. Have the stern paddler step back into the canoe. When seated, both paddlers can shove off from the dam and paddle away.

HUNTER'S STEW

When he meets new people, White Mountains trapper Anton Kaska likes to ask them if they've ever tasted beaver. The answer is usually no, at which point Anton will inform them that castoreum, the musky vanilla-scented goop from under the animal's tail, has been used in foods like ice cream, candy, and booze (like our Tamworth Eau de Musc whiskey) for nearly a hundred years. This easy goulash, from Anton's Hungarian wife, Magdalena, features not castoreum but backstrap, which Anton describes as the filet tips of the beaver meat world. If you find yourself temporarily strapped for backstrap, this recipe works with other wild game (venison, moose) as well as beef chuck.

MAKES 6 TO 8 SERVINGS

¼ cup / 60 ml vegetable oil

1½ medium yellow onions, medium diced

3 medium red bell peppers, medium diced

2 pounds / 1 kg beaver backstrap (or other wild game), cut into 1½ inch / 40 mm cubes

¼ cup / 66 ml tomato paste

⅓ cup / 36 g Hungarian sweet paprika

Cooked egg noodles, for serving

Chopped parsley, for serving

Hang a large Dutch oven on a tripod over a large bed of glowing coals and allow the pot to preheat for 3 minutes. Add the oil and onions and sauté until softened, about 7 minutes. Add the peppers and sauté for 2 minutes. Add the meat and brown on all sides. Remove the pot from the heat and add the tomato paste and paprika, continuously stirring to distribute. Return the pot to the heat and add enough water to cover 3 to 4 inches / 7.5 to 10 cm above the meat. Partially cover the pot so the lid is just off-center and leaves a small gap. Maintain the mixture at a simmer, occasionally stirring and adding coals and water as needed, for 5 to 6 hours, or until the meat is fork-tender. Serve over egg noodles, garnished with parsley.

CONCORD MOON

September and October find vines bulging with grape bunches ready for harvest in southern New Hampshire. Among the varieties is the sweet and juicy Concord, developed by farmer Ephraim Wales Bull in 1849. He named the grape for his adopted hometown—not the capital of New Hampshire but Concord, Massachusetts. A little of that feel-it-in-your-cheeks flavor goes a long way in the Concord Moon, a revisit of the circa 1930s Moon Mist, an obscure Australian potion of gin, maraschino, and grape juice. Barrel-aged gin, which is silkier and sweeter than your standard dry stuff, gives the Concord Moon some weather-appropriate weight. Matched with the puckery sweetness of the grapes and the haunting cherry aroma of the maraschino, it's a cocktail rich in flavor and texture. Save it for a cold autumn night.

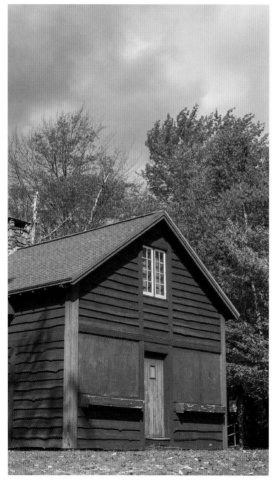

MAKES 1 COCKTAIL

1½ ounces / 45 ml barrel-aged or Old Tom gin

¾ ounce / 22 ml maraschino

½ ounce / 15 ml Concord grape juice

3 dashes aromatic bitters

Garnish: Expressed orange peel

Combine the gin, maraschino, grape juice, and bitters in a mixing glass with ice, briskly stir, and strain into a chilled coupe. Garnish and serve.

FRANCONIA 75

Invented around the first World War, the French 75 is a four-ingredient firework show: gin, lemon, simple syrup, and Champagne. Here is a darker, decidedly New England spin on this classic cocktail: The gin and lemon remain, rich maple syrup dials up the complexity of the sweetness, and hard cider brings bubbles along with a whiff of apple essence. Since the maple will provide all the sugar this cocktail requires, you want a dry cider to maintain balance; Vermont's Shacksbury Dry Cider is a fine option that comes in cans, perfect for camp packing. You can also make a zero-proof version of the Franconia 75 by substituting non alcoholic sparkling apple cider, omitting the maple, and replacing the gin with brewed juniper tea.

MAKES 1 COCKTAIL

1 ounce / 30 ml gin

½ ounce / 15 ml freshly squeezed lemon juice

½ ounce / 15 ml maple syrup

Chilled dry cider to top, about 3 ounces / 90 ml

Garnish: Expressed lemon peel

Combine the gin, lemon juice, and maple syrup in a cocktail shaker with ice and vigorously shake. Strain the cocktail into a tall glass and top with cider. Garnish and serve.

WILD HARE

Carrot juice is an underused cocktail mixer, which makes it such a surprise in the Wild Hare. You see this short, shaken drink, and your eyes tell you "orange juice." But while there is some OJ in here, the overall flavor lives in the savory carrot camp. Mix one up for your friends and watch the confused, then delighted, expression cross their faces. Brisk and dry, the Wild Hare drinks, unexpectedly, like a martini. Against this salt-sharpened, iced-carrot backdrop, a constellation of savory spices comes into focus: fennel, anise, and dill from the aquavit; peppercorn, cinnamon, and cumin from the garam masala bitters. It's an unusual, delicious drink. Have it for a morning pick-me-up or fireside turn-down. Like its namesake, it disappears quickly.

MAKES 1 COCKTAIL

2 ounces / 60 ml aquavit

1 ounce / 30 ml carrot juice

1 ounce / 30 ml freshly squeezed orange juice

Pinch kosher salt

Garnish: 4 drops garam masala bitters, dill sprig

Combine the aquavit, carrot juice, orange juice, and salt in a cocktail shaker with ice and vigorously shake. Strain the cocktail into a short glass over ice, garnish, and serve.

BACKCOUNTRY COCKTAILS

CINNEGRONI

Cinnamon in a negroni? We know; at first it sounds about as appealing as a scorpion in your sleeping bag. Trust us. Fragrant scrolls of cinnamon (and its cousin, cassia) are common flavoring agents in all three of the negroni's key players: gin, amaro, and sweet vermouth. So a cinnamon-forward negroni actually makes a ton of sense, especially for the Autumn. How do we bring the spice to the front? First, by replacing the usual Campari with Averna, an inky amaro heavy on the licorice and spice notes. Then, by steeping toasted cinnamon sticks in a six-count batch of the cocktail. Overnight, those heat-activated essential oils wash the drink in warm, woodsy-sweet cinnamon flavor; you'll smell it as soon as you unscrew the lid.

MAKES 6 COCKTAILS

6 cinnamon sticks

6 ounces / 180 ml gin

6 ounces / 180 ml Averna amaro

6 ounces / 180 ml sweet vermouth

Garnish: Expressed grapefruit peel

Toast the cinnamon sticks in a skillet on the stove, grill, or campfire, occasionally stirring, until fragrant. Place the warm cinnamon in a glass jar and add the gin, Averna, and vermouth. Close and gently shake the jar. Allow it to rest overnight at room temperature. To serve 1 to 5 cocktails: Remove the cinnamon and gently shake the jar to mix. Add 3 ounces / 90 ml per desired number of cocktails to a mixing glass with ice. Stir and strain over fresh ice into short glasses, garnish, and serve. To serve all 6 cocktails: Remove the cinnamon. Add ice directly to the jar, stir, and strain over fresh ice between 6 short glasses. Garnish and serve.

Field Guide:
WILD MUSHROOMS

BY ERIC MILLIGAN

Spring is for morels and Summer for chanterelles, but Autumn is a fungi buffet. You know when you step outside, and it just *smells* like Autumn? That's the smell of the year's greatest concentration of mushrooms fruiting. Foraging from the wild takes a keen eye and a cautious approach to avoid toxic lookalikes. Here are six safe (and scrumptious) varieties you're likely to encounter in the woods of the White Mountains. They overlap with other parts of the country, but always consult local sources, and if you're unsure about a mushroom—or any wild food, really—leave it alone.

BLACK TRUMPET, *CRATERELLUS CORNUCOPIOIDES*

Black funnel-shaped fruitbody with wide gills. The unique smell of this mushroom has deep, earthy tones with iron-y back notes.

Habitat: Grows out of the ground in small groupings. Oak (early Summer) and hemlock (Autumn) are the predominant host associates.

Toxic Lookalikes: None.

Field Notes: With its distinct smell and shape, this is one of the easiest wild mushrooms for beginning foragers to identify. It dries beautifully, and its singular flavor profile lends itself well to both sweet and savory dishes. It also pairs surprisingly well with blueberries.

HEN OF THE WOODS AKA MAITAKE, *GRIFOLA FRONDOSA*

A rosette of brown and gray fronds radiating outwardly from a central basal stalk. White flesh and white pore surface.

Habitat: Grows at the base of hardwoods, most commonly oak and maple. Elm, sycamore, and chestnut can also be host trees.

Toxic Lookalikes: None, though two edible species commonly get misidentified as hen of the woods: black-staining polypore and Berkeley's polypore.

Field Notes: Both tasty and considered by some to be powerfully medicinal. During a good year, huge flushes of this species pop up, and fruitbodies can grow up to 40 to 50 pounds / 18 to 23 kg.

LION'S MANE, *HERICIUM ERINACEUS*

Stalkless, white mass covered with long teeth. Lion's mane has a mild taste and texture akin to shellfish or crabmeat.

Habitat: Grows on dead or dying hardwood trees, predominantly beech and oak.

Toxic Lookalikes: None, though it can sometimes be mistaken with coral mushroom species, which grow out of the ground.

Field Notes: This mushroom tastes best when found in the younger stages of growth. They can become bitter with age.

MATSUTAKE, *TRICHOLOMA MAGNIVELARE*

Round, off-white cap with herringbone patches of light brown and bright white gills. Straight tapering stalk firmly attached to the ground. Young specimens are covered in a veil. The smell of matsutake is the key identifier; it is often described as cinnamon Red Hots candy mixed with dirty feet.

Habitat: Grows singular or in groupings, often forming a fairy ring. Fruits under red pine and hemlock.

Toxic Lookalikes: Matsutake can be mistaken for several deadly *Amanita* species, the destroying angel being the most common, which is why using smell as an identifier is key. Never eat this mushroom before having specimens verified by a trusted identifier.

Field Notes: The prized species is very picky and needs the correct conditions to fruit properly. It's not uncommon for it to skip a year or two of fruiting, especially during a warm, dry Autumn.

OYSTER, *PLEUROTUS OSTREATUS*

Overlapping fan-shaped bodies with decurrent (downward extending) gills and short stem. Color can range from browns and white to bluish gray. Smell is slightly sweet, almost like a cross between anise and shellfish.

Habitat: Grow in brackets directly from dead hardwoods.

Toxic Lookalikes: None, though there are many species that can be misidentified as oysters that would not be considered edible. The key macroscopic features that are always present in oysters are the overlapping smooth caps and decurrent gills.

Field Notes: Look for oyster mushrooms after rainstorms.

PORCINI, *BOLETUS EDULIS* AND RELATED SPECIES: *ATKINSONII, CHIPPEWAENSIS, NOBILIS, SEPARANS, VARIIPES, SUBCAERULESCENS*

Round, reddish-to-tan cap with smooth surface and white pores turning olive in age. The stem is typically tapered with a bulbous base and reticulation (fine netting or webbing pattern) near the top.

Habitat: Grows out of the ground. Depending on subspecies, fir and oak are the most common tree associates.

Toxic Lookalikes: There are no deadly *Bolete* species, but there are dozens that will make you very sick. Eat porcini only if confirmed by a trusted identifier.

Field Notes: Boletes can be quite challenging to properly identify. Up until recent years, the above-listed species were all referred to as *Boletus edulis*. While all of these species share similar attributes, their differences have led to many misidentifications.

LION'S MANE "CRAB CAKES" *with* FERMENTED-RAMP TARTAR SAUCE

When Jamaar Julal finds lion's mane mushrooms (see Field Guide: Wild Mushrooms, page 116) in the woods, he knows exactly what he's making for dinner: crab cakes. Once cooked and shredded, these fungi have a texture that's a dead ringer for crabmeat. Julal serves the vegetarian-friendly cakes with a creamy, wildly flavorful tartar sauce electrified with his fermented ramps (see How to: Ferment Veggies, page 46); try it as a dip for raw veggies or dabbed on a burger. Haven't fermented your ramps yet? Fresh ones are also delicious in this sauce.

MAKES 5 TO 6 SERVINGS

CAKES

1 pound / 450 g lion's mane mushrooms, shredded by hand into crabmeat-sized pieces

¼ cup / 60 ml water

½ teaspoon Diamond Crystal (or ¼ teaspoon Morton) kosher salt, plus more to taste

2 large eggs, beaten

¼ cup / 60 ml mayonnaise

2 tablespoons Dijon mustard

1 tablespoon Worcestershire sauce

¼ cup / 60 g thinly sliced scallions

1 teaspoon Old Bay seasoning

½ teaspoon black pepper

1¼ cups / 100 g panko breadcrumbs or crushed saltine crackers, divided

Olive oil, for searing

Lemon wedges, for garnish

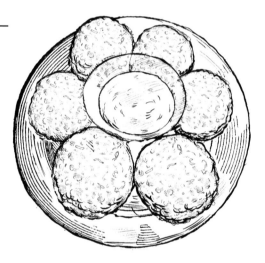

TARTAR SAUCE

6 lacto-fermented ramps (see How to: Ferment Veggies, page 46)

2 cups / 470 ml mayonnaise

3 tablespoons minced dill

Juice and zest of 1 lemon

Kosher salt and black pepper, to taste

Combine the shredded mushrooms, water, and salt in a medium pot on the stove, grill, or campfire. Cover the pot and bring the mixture to a simmer, occasionally stirring, until the mushrooms have released their moisture, about 3 to 5 minutes. (Depending on the size of your pot, you may want to do this in 2 batches.)

Strain out the mushrooms and set them on a clean dish towel to cool. When completely cooled, gather the corners of the towel into a bundle and thoroughly wring out as much excess liquid as possible from the mushrooms. The less leftover moisture, the better and more "crabby" the texture of the cakes.

Combine the mushrooms with the eggs, mayonnaise, mustard, Worcestershire sauce, scallions, Old Bay, pepper, and half of the breadcrumbs in a large bowl. Thoroughly mix the ingredients until fully incorporated and taste for seasoning, adding salt if needed. Chill the mixture in the fridge or cooler for at least 20 minutes and up to overnight, covering the bowl with plastic if chilling longer than 1 hour. By hand or with ring molds, form the mixture into cakes that are roughly 1 inch / 2.5 cm thick. You should get 10 to 12 cakes.

Add enough oil to cover the bottom of a large pan, about 3 tablespoons, and set it over medium heat. While the pan is heating, evenly dredge the cakes in the remaining breadcrumbs. Working in 2 batches, gently sear the cakes in the oil until golden brown, about 3 minutes on each side.

While the cakes are cooking, make the tartar sauce. Place the ramps in a paper towel or piece of cheesecloth, bundle, and squeeze to wring out any brine. Mince the ramps and combine them with the mayonnaise, dill, lemon juice and zest, salt, and pepper in a medium bowl. Whisk together until evenly incorporated. Serve the sauce alongside the finished cakes.

GINGERYE

This tall, thirst-quenching refresher sets off down a familiar autumn cocktail trail—a little whiskey, a little ginger, a little cider—then takes a detour and stumbles onto a hidden grotto of beer. The crisp bitterness of an IPA makes a fantastic foil to the sweetness and spice of the other ingredients. Think of the Gingerye as a boilermaker on a New Hampshire camping trip.

MAKES 1 COCKTAIL

1 ounce / 30 ml ginger liqueur

½ ounce / 15 ml rye whiskey

¾ ounce / 22 ml apple cider

½ ounce / 15 ml freshly squeezed lemon juice

IPA to top, about 3 ounces / 90 ml

Garnish: Ginger slice

Combine the ginger liqueur, whiskey, cider, and lemon juice in a tall glass with ice and stir to combine. Top with the beer, garnish, and serve.

APPLESEED SOUR

Most cocktails in the sour family have a single-spirit base: whiskey sour, rum sour, and so on. The Appleseed Sour dreams bigger, with Calvados and mezcal weaving a poem of oak, smoke, apple, and caramel. Honey provides a richer sweetness than the usual simple syrup, and tahini introduces savory sesame action to this all-star sour.

MAKES 1 COCKTAIL

1¼ ounces / 40 ml Calvados

¾ ounce / 22 ml mezcal

½ ounce / 15 ml Honey Syrup (see page 90)

½ ounce / 15 ml tahini

½ ounce / 15 ml freshly squeezed lemon juice

White from 1 large egg or 1 ounce / 30 ml aquafaba

Garnish: Expressed lemon peel

Combine the Calvados, mezcal, syrup, tahini, lemon juice, and egg white in a cocktail shaker and vigorously shake for 30 seconds. Add ice and shake again. Strain the cocktail into a short glass over ice, garnish, and serve.

GHOST IN THE SIDECAR

Apples hog most of the attention in the orchard. Pity the pear? Nah. New England's *other* autumn fruit gets its due in this take on a sidecar. In lieu of the usual Cognac, all golden and boastful and barreled, pear brandy plays base. This eau de vie—Poire Williams from Alsace is the most common brand—is clear and pure, in appearance as well as aromatic expression of the fruit. In other words, a ghost you can sense without seeing. Pear nectar and pear bitters enhance it, with Grand Marnier and lemon reprising their citrusy roles. This is a smooth, ever-so-slightly sweet sipper. If you're staying in a cabin with glassware, we like it in a coupe, per sidecar tradition, but it's just as delectable strained into any unfussy cup.

MAKES 1 COCKTAIL

1½ ounces / 45 ml pear brandy

½ ounce / 15 ml Grand Marnier

1 ounce / 30 ml pear nectar

½ ounce / 15 ml freshly squeezed lemon juice

Garnish: Pear wheel, 3 drops pear bitters

Combine the brandy, Grand Marnier, pear nectar, and lemon juice in a mixing glass with ice and briskly stir. Strain into a chilled coupe, garnish, and serve.

Field Guide:
DEER TRACKING

BY ANTON KASKA

Whether hunting deer for food or photographs, it's not a task for the impatient. But these swift and evasive creatures leave plenty of breadcrumbs, particularly during the rut (mating season) in November. Pack your meditative mindset and follow the signs.

WATER: In drier areas, one of the easiest places to pick up deer signs is on runs and paths near water. Begin tracking here.

FOOTPRINTS: Whitetail deer have pointy toes, usually between 1¼ and 4 inches / 3 to 10 cm in length. These leave behind a pair of almost heart-shaped impacts for each foot, with the pointy ends pointing in the forward direction of travel.

BUMPS: If you see an increase in the length of stride, you may have bumped or surprised the deer, causing it to run.

SCRAPES: Male deer often make scrapes during the rut (autumn months). In a forest or wooded environment, they are simply scrapes in the dirt made by the hooves, which clear away leaves and debris. The buck will urinate in this scraped area as a sign for any receptive does and to let other bucks know of his presence. Often there are small boughs over this scrape area, which show signs of disturbance.

RUBS: Rubs are small trees and saplings the buck rubs hard with his antlers when moving along his route, trying to find receptive does. These will have the bark literally rubbed clean off, and sometimes larger bucks will break the sapling in half.

HAIRS: Deer often leave hairs on brush when moving through very heavy growth. Look for them on bushes and branches.

SCAT: This is common, so look for it in areas with heavy cover, where deer may be sleeping, and on sunny slopes, where deer will lie and warm themselves.

SUCCOTASH

BY DENISE AND PAUL POULIOT,
COWASUCK BAND OF THE PENNACOOK-ABENAKI PEOPLE

Succotash is an Algonquin Indigenous word from the Narragansett Indian Tribe of Rhode Island, from the original *sohquttahhash*, meaning "broken corn kernels." In the Abenaki language it's called *ns8b8n* (corn soup), and within the greater Northeast Indigenous community it has always been any dish that contains both corn (*skamonal*) and beans (*adebakwal*). Once you have those staples, you can freestyle the rest, adding Indigenous vegetables like fiddlehead ferns (*masozial*) and sunchokes (*wiz8watwal wajapkwol*) or meats (*wiosal*), though as written this recipe is completely vegan. Abenaki names appear in italics next to the English. The *8* sound is pronounced like ô.

MAKES 8 SERVINGS

4 cans (60 ounces / 1.7 kg) whole-kernel sweet corn (*skamonal*)

1 can (15 ounces / 425 g) pinto beans (*adebakwal*)

1 can (15 ounces / 425 g) kidney or lima beans (*adebakwal*)

½ cup / 26 g coarsely chopped onion or scallions (*winozak*)

2 red potatoes (*padatesak*), with skin, coarsely diced

4 cups / 1 L water (*nebi*) or vegetable broth to cover

Kosher salt (*siwan*) and black pepper (*tipwabel*), to taste

Combine all the ingredients in a large pot, including the liquid in the corn and bean cans. Bring the mixture to a boil over medium-high heat on the stove, grill, or campfire. Reduce the heat to maintain a high simmer until the potatoes are cooked through, about 20 minutes. Season to taste and serve.

CRANBERRY BUCK

The buck (aka mule) is not a single cocktail but a choose-your-own-adventure drink. The constants are citrus juice and ginger ale or ginger beer, while the spirit is the drinker's choice. A gin buck is gin, citrus, and ginger. A bourbon buck is bourbon, citrus, and ginger. You get the idea. On warm autumn afternoons, we're fixing bubbly, burgundy Cranberry Bucks to rest on the arms of our Adirondack chairs. Vodka is the base, a neutral background on which the tart cranberry and spicy ginger can shine. Be sure to use cranberry juice, not cranberry cocktail, for this recipe. If you can only find the latter, which is heavily sweetened, nix the syrup.

MAKES 1 COCKTAIL

2 ounces / 60 ml vodka

¾ ounce / 22 ml cranberry juice

½ ounce / 15 ml freshly squeezed lime juice

½ ounce / 15 ml Simple Syrup (see Violet Fizz, page 22)

Ginger beer to top, about 2 ounces / 60 ml

Garnish: Lime wedge

Combine the vodka, cranberry juice, lime juice, and syrup in a cocktail shaker with ice and vigorously shake. Strain the cocktail into a tall glass over ice and top with the ginger beer. Gently stir just to incorporate, garnish, and serve.

JACK-O'-LANTERN

Every Autumn, pumpkin spice emerges from the underworld for its seasonal crusade. Even out in the mountains, it's inescapable. So instead of closing our collection of autumn cocktails with a saccharine goodbye, here's a spiced-pumpkin dessert drink that doesn't taste like it came from Starbucks. The Jack-O'-Lantern contains *actual* pumpkin—a can of puree makes for easy packing—and gets its hints of cinnamon, vanilla, and allspice from spiced rum, while amaretto brings its unexpected sweet-almond essence. With lemon and bitters to balance, it's part Pilgrim, part pirate, and wholly unlike any pumpkin cocktail out there.

MAKES 1 COCKTAIL

Lemon wedge

Brown sugar, for rimming the glass

1½ ounces / 45 ml spiced rum

1 ounce / 30 ml amaretto

1 ounce / 30 ml pumpkin puree

½ ounce / 15 ml freshly squeezed lemon juice

2 dashes aromatic bitters

Rub half of the rim of a chilled coupe with a lemon wedge and dip it into brown sugar. Place the glass right side up. Combine the rum, amaretto, pumpkin puree, lemon juice, and bitters in a cocktail shaker with ice and vigorously shake. Strain the cocktail into the prepared glass and serve.

ALPINE COCOA

Over in the French Alps, the ski-and-be-seen chalet crowd thaws out with verte chaud, the "hot green" warmer made by spiking cocoa with green Chartreuse. You can use Chartreuse in this recipe, but we like Dolin's Génépy le Chamois for its delicately piney-vanilla bouquet, a beautiful match for chocolate. The method below outlines making the cocoa to order, but you can also prepare it in advance and store it in an insulated thermos; it's a perfect companion for a winter walk.

MAKES 4 COCKTAILS

1 quart / 1 L whole milk

¼ cup / 25 g cocoa powder

¼ cup / 50 g granulated sugar

1 tablespoon ground instant coffee or espresso

Pinch cinnamon, plus more for garnish

Pinch kosher salt

1 cup / 240 ml Génépy le Chamois or green Chartreuse

Garnish: Whipped cream, grated dark chocolate

Whisk the milk and cocoa together in a medium pot to begin to dissolve the cocoa. Set it over medium heat on the stove, grill, or campfire and bring it to a simmer. Add the sugar, coffee, cinnamon, and salt and continue to simmer, briskly whisking to dissolve the sugar and any clumps, until the cocoa is slightly foamy and hot to the touch. Divide the cocoa between 4 mugs, add 2 ounces / 60 ml Génépy de Chamois to each, and stir. Garnish with whipped cream, chocolate, and cinnamon and serve.

Family Style: Add all the génépy to the pot of hot cocoa and stir. Add a ladle for self-serving.

BY LEE NOBLE

For warmth, for cooking, for trading fables and ghost stories, or for sipping coffee and cocktails, the fire is the heart of the campsite, and building a sturdy, self-sustaining, *safe* blaze is an absolutely essential skill. This guide makes two assumptions: (1) you're at an established campsite—whether it's a private campground, national park, or the like—where there are designated fire areas, often indicated by a conspicuous ring or pit dug into the ground, and (2) you're creating your fire the old-fashioned, gentler way, without accelerants like lighter fluid and newspaper.

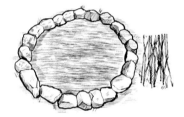

1. Clear any unburnt logs or sticks out of the fire pit and place them to the side. They may still be useful once your fire is going.

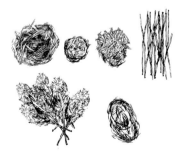

2. Select your firewood. The best fire starts before a match is struck, which means the quality and selection of your firewood is the key to a successful fire. Three categories of flammable materials should be found and organized before starting the fire: tinder, kindling, and fuel.

Tinder is used to start the fire. It's the light, easily collected and lit forest debris: dried leaves, twigs, downed birch bark, fatwood, dried punk wood, dried pine needles, or generally any small, dried-out vegetation. Do not pick live plants, as this is destructive to the campground, not to mention they don't burn well.

Kindling is ignited by the tinder and used to make the fire hot enough to burn the fuel. It's bigger than tinder but not as big as fuel. Look for downed sticks and small branches that aren't much thicker than your thumb and break them into pieces the length of your forearm. Larger pieces of birch bark, fatwood, and punk wood may also qualify as kindling.

Fuel is what we commonly think of as logs, but on the smaller side. Pieces should come from dead and dried wood, never live cuttings, and be no thicker or longer than your forearm. They may need to be cut down to fit in the firepit, so a small camp saw would be a useful tool to bring along. The size consideration is important to ensure the fire starts quickly, stays small and easy to control, and is also easy to extinguish at the end of the night.

3. To start building the fire, place a pile of tinder, enough to overflow your two hands cupped together, in the middle of the firepit.

4. Use the longer sticks of kindling to build a teepee shape around the tinder by leaning the sticks up against each other at an angle. This is a balancing act and may take some skill and patience. Usually 8 to 10 sticks are a good start for a small campfire. As you build, be sure the tinder is still exposed to lots of air and is accessible so that you can light it when the time comes. On that note, leave plenty of room for air to move in and around the kindling as well, as the fire needs air to breathe in order to burn hot. In other words, you will suffocate the newly lit fire if the sticks are packed too tightly.

5. Using a match or a lighter, ignite the tinder and wait for it to set the kindling on fire. Depending on the conditions, you will likely need to add more tinder to get the kindling going. This could take just a few minutes or as long as 10 or 15 minutes, depending on conditions.

6. As the kindling begins to burn hot, try adding a few more pieces at a time to build up to the heat needed to ignite the fuel. This step often takes 10 minutes or more.

7. Once the kindling is burning independently without the need to add more to keep it going, add some of your fuel. Place 3 or 4 small logs in the shape of a teepee over the heart of the fire to allow air circulation. (You may need to add more kindling during this step to keep the fire growing.)

8. After some time, often another 10 or 15 minutes, you should see that most of the tinder and kindling has become a hotbed of coals at the heart of the fire, and the fuel logs are burning hot over it. They may have even collapsed into the center, which is okay, as long as they're still burning well. Once a stable fire has been built, you may add more logs as needed, being mindful not to build it taller than knee high or outside of the fire pit.

9. Be sure the fire is completely extinguished before you go to bed for the night. Not a single cinder should be left burning. This helps prevent forest fires, as well as other emergencies, like a flying ember landing on your tent after you've fallen asleep. You may need to douse the fire with water for several minutes in order to put it out completely.

RED WINE WASSAIL

Wassail is an old-timey British verb for holiday caroling. You know the song: "Here we come a-caroling among the leaves so green . . ." The American lyrics substitute *a-caroling* for the original *a-wassailing.* When wassailing on Christmas Eve, residents would traditionally serve the roaming carolers a fortifying pour of warm spiced cider, ale, or wine. Over time, this concoction also came to be known as wassail. Our red wine–based recipe doesn't require a holiday. All you need is any frosty winter night and a little patience. The wassail won't smell like much at first, but over the course of an hour, as the spices and apples simmer away in the wine, a heady yuletide fragrance—and festive vibe—will settle over your kitchen or campsite. If you find yourself inclined to organize a singalong, all the better. Just don't forget those original lyrics: "Love and joy, come to you, and to you your wassail, too!"

MAKES 4 TO 6 COCKTAILS

6 allspice berries

4 cloves

4 cardamom pods

2 cinnamon sticks

2 star anise

1 (750 ml) bottle of pinot noir or other light-bodied red wine

½ cup / 120 ml cream sherry

1 small apple, sliced crossways

½ cup / 100 g granulated sugar

Toast the allspice, cloves, cardamom, cinnamon sticks, and anise in a large pot over low heat on the stove, grill, or campfire, occasionally stirring until fragrant, about 5 minutes. Add the wine and sherry and increase the heat to bring the mixture to a rolling simmer. Add the apple, reduce the heat to very low, and allow the mixture to cook at a bare simmer until very fragrant and reduced by roughly half, 45 minutes to 1 hour. Remove the pot from the heat and add the sugar, stirring until completely dissolved. Strain out and reserve the spices and apples and divide the wassail between mugs. Garnish with the reserved spices and apples and serve.

Family Style: Do not strain the wassail. Leave the pot on very low heat and add a ladle for self-serving.

FLANNEL SHEETS

Two Cognac cocktails walk into a cabin. Between the Sheets says to Flannel, "I wish I had some of your spice." Flannel counters, "I wish I had some of your rum." The rest is history, wrapped up in cozy plaid. Like the titular sheets, this drink will keep you warm through the coldest winter nights.

MAKES 1 COCKTAIL

1 ounce / 30 ml Cognac

1 ounce / 30 ml light rum

½ ounce / 15 ml allspice dram

½ ounce / 15 ml Grand Marnier

¼ ounce / 7 ml freshly squeezed lemon juice

¼ ounce / 7 ml Simple Syrup (see Violet Fizz, page 22)

Garnish: Expressed orange peel

Combine the Cognac, rum, allspice dram, Grand Marnier, lemon juice, and syrup in a cocktail shaker with ice and vigorously shake. Strain the cocktail into a short glass over ice, garnish, and serve.

MAPLE SLUSH

New Hampshire ranks third in the country in average annual snowfall and seventh in maple syrup production. This cocktail brings those two Winter-in-the-Whites traditions together, with maple syrup and aquavit, the caraway-scented Scandinavian firewater, poured over a mound of fresh, fluffy snow. Stirred together, the trio melds into a tawny slush as bracing as a nor'easter. It's key to collect snow that has just fallen, and even then, only the top layer—pebbles, sticks, and other forest-floor detritus taste terrible, you know? If there's no precipitation in the forecast (or you live somewhere with high levels of air pollution), this recipe works just as well with shaved ice.

MAKES 1 COCKTAIL

2 ounces / 60 ml aquavit

4 ounces / 120 ml maple syrup

2 cups / 500 ml freshly fallen clean snow (or substitute finely shaved ice)

Stir the aquavit and maple syrup together in a mixing glass. Fill a mug with the snow, mounding it on top to form a dome, and drizzle the aquavit-maple mixture over top. Serve with a spoon.

How to:
TAP A MAPLE

BY STEVE BARTLETT

Successfully tapping a maple is very dependent on weather; ideal weather is well below freezing at night and up into the 40s during the day. Without the temperature swings you don't get the pressure, which is what gets the sap moving. In New Hampshire, those swings are most consistent in the second week of March, which we call "the hero-making part of the season." Once the weather's right, all you need are a tree, a drill, a spout, and a bucket to be on your way to your very own cuvée of maple syrup.

1. First make sure you're not on privately owned land, and then find a sugar maple. A good tree guide will help you identify the sugar maple's characteristic leaf shape. A tree with a healthy crown and a trunk at least 10 to 12 inches / 25 to 30 cm in diameter is a good specimen for tapping.

2. Give the tree a hug. This is how we determine if the tree can take one or two taps. If your hands meet, place one tap only. If they don't meet, two will work.

3. Using a cordless power drill fitted with a ⁷/₁₆-in / 19 mm bit, drill gently into the trunk to initiate a hole, then bore in at a slight upward angle, about 1½ to 1³/₄ inches / 4 to 4.5 cm deep.

4. Tap the tree using a hook and spile (maple tapping spout). Push the spile into the drilled hole and tap it into place with a hammer. (If you're double-tapping the tree, place the second spile on the opposite side of the trunk.)

5. Place the hook on the spile and hang a bucket from it. The spile will run continuously or intermittently, depending on the weather during the day.

6. When you've collected at least 2 gallons / 7.5 L of sap, transfer it to a large pot and bring it to a boil. Continuously boil, maintaining 219°F / 104°C on a candy thermometer, until reduced to about 1 cup / 250 ml and the syrup coats the back of a spoon.

7. Use the syrup immediately or transfer it to a glass or plastic quart jar or other sturdy container and store in the fridge.

ENERGY BARS, TWO WAYS

Cabin:
SESAME MAPLE GRANOLA BARS

If you have access to an oven and some basic equipment—or are baking before a trip—a fresh batch of these nutty, multi-textured, maple-and-date-sweetened bars will be ready in under an hour. The flavor is more interesting than that of the usual mass-produced bars, thanks to the savory edge of tahini, a burst of fresh orange, and enough salt to notice.

MAKES 12 BARS

1 cup / 135 g hazelnuts

1 cup / 120 g pecans

2 cups / 150 g rolled old-fashioned oats

2 tablespoons chia seeds

2 teaspoons cinnamon

2 teaspoons Diamond Crystal (or 1 teaspoon Morton) kosher salt

2 teaspoons avocado (or other neutral) oil, plus more for oiling your hands

12 pitted dates, roughly chopped

Zest from 2 large oranges

½ cup / 120 ml maple syrup

¾ cup / 200 g tahini

Whites from 2 large eggs

Sea salt, to taste

Preheat the oven to 350°F. Toast the hazelnuts and pecans on a quarter-sheet (or other small) pan until toasty and fragrant, about 10 minutes. Remove and allow them to cool. Meanwhile, combine the oats, chia, cinnamon, salt, oil, dates, and orange zest in a large mixing bowl. When the nuts are cool enough to handle, finely chop half and roughly chop the other half. (This will create multiple textures throughout the bars.) Add the chopped nuts to the oat mixture. Heat the maple syrup in a small saucepan over low heat until just warm and bubbling around the edges. Pour the maple syrup over the tahini and whisk to combine, then add it to the oat mixture.

Get out 2 quarter-sheet pans and 2 sheets of parchment paper slightly larger than the pans. Line one pan with parchment and reserve the other.

Lightly oil your hands and thoroughly mix the oat mixture. Add the egg whites and continue to mix until everything is well combined. The mixture should loosely clump together when squeezed. Turn it out onto the prepared pan and spread it out as evenly as possible. Place the second piece of parchment on top, followed by the second pan, and firmly press down to create a flat, even layer. Remove the top pan and top piece of parchment and dust the bars with sea salt. Bake for 35 to 40 minutes, until the bars are firm and the edges appear crunchy and brown.

Remove the bars from the oven and allow them to cool for 20 minutes. Cut them into 12 equal pieces and allow them to continue to cool at room temperature until fully set but still slightly flexible. Wrap them individually in plastic and store in an airtight container to preserve the chewy texture. For crunchier bars, leave them out at room temperature for an extra day before packing. Either way, they'll keep for a couple weeks.

Camp: PEMMIGAN

BY DENISE AND PAUL POULIOT,
COWASUCK BAND OF THE PENNACOOK-ABENAKI PEOPLE

A favorite of the kids at our crafting workshops, pemmigan is the original energy bar and requires zero baking. In Abenaki, the root language of all Algonquin dialects, *pemmi* refers to fat, oil, or grease derived from bear, deer, moose, or possibly whale, while the word ending *-gan* refers to a thing that is made. Ancient pemmigan recipes featured raw venison or other meats pounded into a paste with vegetables, fruits, and Indigenous plants, but this contemporary version is completely vegan, with a mixture of nuts and seeds supplying all the fats necessary to create a nutritious, delicious snack. You can mix in any other nuts, seeds, or dried fruits you like, but this recipe contains all Native produce (except pecans, which we find to be a suitable substitution for butternuts).

MAKES 12 SERVINGS

½ cup / 50 g raw walnuts (*pedeg8menoziak*)

½ cup / 55 g raw pecans

½ cup / 60 g raw pumpkin seeds (*wasawal*)

½ cup / 60 g dried blueberries (*zatal*)

½ cup / 70 g dried sweet or sour cherries (*kchi adebimenal*)

½ cup / 65 g dried cranberries (*popokwaimenal*)

½ cup / 70 g dried strawberries (*mskioiminsak*)

Combine the ingredients in a mortar (*ad8kwigan*) and grind them with a pestle (*gwenasenakw*) until the nut and seed oils release and begin to combine with the fruit pulp. You may need to do this in batches, depending on the size of your mortar. (No mortar and pestle? You can also use a zip-top bag and the bottom of a cast-iron skillet, a rolling pin, or even a rock.) Continue to work the mixture until it is thoroughly combined and the appearance is mostly uniform; it should be sticky and pliable.

Scrape the mixture onto a large piece of waxed paper or plastic wrap, roll the paper/wrap over the mixture, and shape the pemmigan into a log using gentle hand pressure. Cut into 12 equal pieces and wrap them individually in plastic wrap. They'll keep at room temperature for weeks but can also be stored in the fridge indefinitely.

DAMSON NEGRONI

A nutty, aromatic negroni born of the harvest and poured for the holidays, starring gin infused with inky-blue damson plums. We make our own, Tamworth Garden Damson Gin, but if you can't get here to pick up a bottle of this lovely magenta spirit, high-quality sloe gin makes a fine substitute, or you can add a tablespoon of plum preserves to the recipe. The black walnut bitters are a tiny addition with an outsized influence on the overall flavor of this negroni, so it's worth the extra effort to find a bottle. Fee Brothers is the most widely available brand.

MAKES 1 COCKTAIL

1½ ounces / 45 ml plum gin (or substitute sloe gin)

¾ ounce / 22 ml Campari

¾ ounce / 22 ml sweet vermouth

2 dashes black walnut bitters

Garnish: Orange peel

Combine the gin, Campari, vermouth, and bitters in a mixing glass with ice and briskly stir. Strain into a short glass over ice, garnish, and serve.

FIVE-SPICED POM TODDY

In Greece, revelers welcome each new year by smashing a pomegranate, an ancient symbol of rebirth and fertility. In the White Mountains, we brew pomegranate tea—same flavor, less mess—and turn it into a bright, fragrant toddy with gin, lime, and syrup spiced with cinnamon, star anise, clove, fennel, and Sichuan peppercorn. If you don't have the setup or planning wherewithal to make the Five Spice Syrup separately, you can also make this toddy in a single space-and-time-saving pot. Just follow the alternate instructions at the end of the recipe.

MAKES 1 COCKTAIL

1 cup / 240 ml boiling water

1 pomegranate teabag

2 ounces / 60 ml gin

1½ ounces / 45 ml Five Spice Syrup

½ ounce / 15 ml freshly squeezed lime juice

Garnish: Lime wheel

Brew the tea in a mug to desired strength. Add the gin, syrup, and lime juice. Stir to combine, garnish, and serve.

One-Pot Pom Toddy (for Two)

Toast double the amount of spices listed in the Five Spice Syrup recipe and steep in 2 cups / 470 ml of water for 30 minutes. Set up 2 mugs, each with a pomegranate teabag and granulated sugar to taste. Return the water to a boil and strain it into the prepared mugs. Allow the tea to brew to the desired strength, then add 2 ounces / 60 ml of gin and ½ ounce / 15 ml of lime juice to each mug. Stir, garnish, and serve.

FIVE SPICE SYRUP

MAKES 1 CUP / 240 ML

3 cinnamon sticks

6 cloves

4 star anise

1 teaspoon fennel seeds

1 teaspoon Sichuan peppercorns

¾ cup / 180 ml water

¾ cup / 150 g granulated sugar

Toast the cinnamon, cloves, anise, fennel, and peppercorns in a saucepot over low heat on the stove, grill, or campfire, occasionally stirring until fragrant, about 5 minutes. Add the water and bring the mixture to a simmer. Remove it from the heat, cover the pot, and allow the spices to steep for 10 minutes. Add the sugar and whisk to completely dissolve. Cover the pot and allow the syrup to cool for 30 minutes. Strain out the spices, transfer the syrup to a jar, and store cold until ready to use.

PINE COLLINS

Zirbenz is an ancient liqueur made from the cones of skyscraper stone pines that carpet the Austrian Alps, but spiritually it feels part and parcel with our mountains on the other side of the world. Woodsy and minty, sweet and fresh, the complex flavor lets it stand on its own as a digestive, but Zirbenz also shows well in this Collins format. Lemon, bitters, and a long pull of seltzer stretch out the sweetness and give the cocktail lift, taking the liqueur from after-dinner to happy hour.

MAKES 1 COCKTAIL

1½ ounces / 45 ml Zirbenz pine liqueur

¾ ounce / 22 ml freshly squeezed lemon juice

¼ ounce / 7 ml Simple Syrup (see Violet Fizz, page 22)

3 dashes aromatic bitters

Seltzer to top, about 3 ounces / 90 ml

Garnish: Pine sprig

Fill a tall glass with ice. Add the Zirbenz, lemon juice, syrup, and bitters and briskly stir to combine. Top with seltzer and stir, garnish, and serve.

COCONUT HAMP NOG

Most modern eggnog recipes assume would-be revelers have a blender or mixer on hand, but unless you're ensconced in a fully kitted-out cabin, it's unlikely those are available on a camping trip. The *Backcountry Cocktails* way assumes only the most basic tools are available: Got a whisk and a bowl in your pack? This festive, frothy, silky eggnog is attainable with just a little elbow grease.

MAKES 4 COCKTAILS

4 large eggs

4 teaspoons granulated sugar

4 teaspoons maple syrup

6 ounces / 180 ml full-fat unsweetened coconut milk

6 ounces / 180 ml bourbon

6 dashes chocolate or mole bitters

Garnish: Grated nutmeg

Vigorously whisk the eggs, sugar, and maple syrup in a bowl until well incorporated. Slowly add the coconut milk, continuously whisking, followed by the bourbon and bitters. Whisk to completely combine. Garnish and serve in short glasses over ice or chill for at least 30 minutes before garnishing and serving straight up.

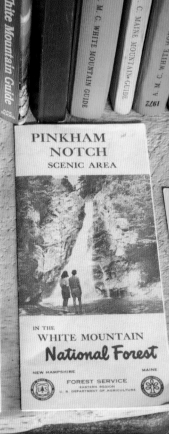

SALTED CARAMEL FLIP

This is a dessert cocktail. Or is it? A member of the egg-enriched flip family, this whiskey-spiked caramel shake is comforting, like shrugging into a shearling-lined sleeping bag. Texturally, it's completely decadent. But the sweetness is surprisingly restrained, with two strong ounces of spicy rye plus the citrus and salt all working to balance the caramel. Since you'll probably have to bring along a whole jar of caramel sauce, you can easily scale up and batch this recipe to use it up. Just be sure to leave out the eggs and add them only when you're ready to shake.

MAKES 1 COCKTAIL

2 ounces / 60 ml rye whiskey

¾ ounce / 22 ml freshly squeezed lemon juice

½ ounce / 15 ml prepared salted caramel sauce

1 large egg

Garnish: Sea salt, grated nutmeg

Combine the whiskey, lemon juice, caramel sauce, and egg in a cocktail shaker and vigorously shake for a full minute to completely incorporate the egg. Add ice and shake again. Strain the cocktail into a short glass, garnish, and serve.

MONT BLANC

The name of this pale jade drink is French for *White Mountain*. We're not saying it was fate that we discovered it in 1935's *Old Waldorf-Astoria Bar Book*, but we're not *not* saying that. The original formula calls for one pony of orgeat, one jigger of absinthe, white of one egg . . . and chilled seltzer. It is in essence a fizz, minus the citrus. Our version maintains the voluminous foam of the Waldorf's but introduces hints of chocolate and rosemary to the profile of almond and licorice. Brisk, camphorous, and not too sweet, the Mont Blanc works as well as a pick-me-up after a rigorous winter hike or as a leisurely after-dinner drink by the fireplace.

MAKES 1 COCKTAIL

1½ ounces / 45 ml absinthe

1 ounce / 30 ml orgeat syrup

½ ounce / 15 ml white crème de cacao

White from 1 large egg or 1 ounce / 30 ml aquafaba

Seltzer to top, about 3 ounces / 90 ml

Garnish: Rosemary sprig

Combine the absinthe, orgeat, crème de cacao, and egg white in a cocktail shaker and vigorously shake to whip the egg white. Add ice and shake again. Strain into a tall glass over crushed ice, top with seltzer, garnish, and serve.

CAMP COFFEE

The hallmark of traditional whiskey-spiked Irish coffee is its tall toque of beaten cream, which is impressive and delicious and . . . not super feasible in the context of camping. Sweetened condensed milk (traditional in Vietnamese coffee) provides a nifty work-around. It comes in a small can, is easy to pack, and does the job of creaming and sweetening the coffee in one shot. Camp Coffee is a true day-to-night drink. Fill up a thermos to fortify you for a snowy morning hike or unwind with a mug after dinner.

MAKES 4 COCKTAILS

¼ cup / 25 g coarsely ground coffee beans

4 cups / 1 L boiling water

1 cup / 250 ml Irish whiskey

Sweetened condensed milk, to taste

Brew the coffee in a French press or kettle to desired strength and divide it between 4 mugs. Add 2 ounces / 60 ml whiskey to each mug and stir to combine. Add the milk to taste, stir to combine, and serve.

BROWN BUTTERED RUM

Hot buttered rum is as old as the American colonies. *Brown* Buttered Rum is now. It involves an extra step—browning the butter—but the effort is worth it for the nutty, toasty layer of flavor it brings to the drink. Once browned with cinnamon, cardamom, and vanilla, the butter gets blended with brown sugar into a batter. When you pour the hot water and rum over top, the batter melts, releasing fragrant whiffs of sweet spice that will get the attention of everyone around the campfire.

MAKES 6 COCKTAILS

1 stick / 110 g salted butter

2 teaspoons ground cinnamon

1 teaspoon ground cardamom or 6 cardamom pods

1 split vanilla bean or 1 teaspoon vanilla extract

5 cups / 1.2 L water

1½ cups / 350 ml dark rum

½ cup / 100 g light or dark brown sugar

Garnish: Cinnamon sticks

Melt the butter in a small skillet over low heat on the stove, grill, or campfire. Add the cinnamon, cardamom, and vanilla. Swirling the skillet occasionally, continue to heat the mixture until it becomes brown and foamy, and smells nutty and toasty, about 6 minutes. Remove the butter from the heat and allow it to cool and slightly resolidify in the skillet.

While the butter is cooling, bring the water to a boil. Remove the water from the heat and let it stand for 5 minutes before adding the rum and stirring to combine.

Remove and discard the vanilla bean and whole cardamom pods (if using) from the cooled brown butter. Mix in the brown sugar until well incorporated; the texture should be like wet sand. Divide the mixture between 6 mugs and top each with the water-rum mixture. Garnish and serve.

Family Style: Combine the batter and all of the water and rum in a serving pot and stir. Add a ladle for self-serving.

It Takes a Village ...

Daniela Fedorowicz, Maddie Heenan, and Jenn Bakos photographed *Backcountry Cocktails.*

Neal Santos provided additional photography. Prop styling by Jackie Nevin.

Any images not shot with a camera were illustrated by the legendary Ron Short, with key assistance from Jimmy Shin.

Art direction was by Kevin Flagler (and Arlo Flagler).

New Hampshire fixer, fact-checker, and fireplace tender: Jillian Anderson

Moral and logistical support: Andrew Campbell

Title conjuring and manuscript proofing: Sonia Grasse

Distillery unit: Matt Power

Book design by Quaker City Mercantile and Amanda Richmond of Running Press

Edited with care and joy by Shannon Fabricant of Running Press, with production editing by Melanie Gold and copy editing by Lori Paximadis.

Authors represented by Clare Pelino of Pro Literary Consultant.

Index